SONGS OF THE GOSPEL

1 THE LORD'S MY SHEPHERD

By kind permission.

Scottish Psalter, 1650

JAMES EDMUND JONES

mf 1. The Lord's my Shep - herd, I'll not want, He makes me
2. My soul He doth re - store a - gain, And me to
mp 3. Yea, though I walk in death's dark vale, Yet will I
mf 4. My ta - ble Thou hast fur - nish - ed In pres - ence
5. Good - ness and mer - cy all my life Shall sure - ly

down to lie In pas - tures green; He lead - eth me The
walk doth make With - in the paths of right - eous - ness, Ev'n
fear no ill; *cr.* For Thou art with me, and Thy rod And
of my foes; My head Thou dost with oil a - noint, And
fol - low me, *cr.* And in God's house for ev - er - more My

qui - et wa - ters by, The qui - et wa - ters by.
for His own name's sake, Ev'n for His own name's sake.
staff me com - fort still, And staff me com - fort still.
my cup o - ver - flows, And my cup o - ver - flows.
dwell-ing-place shall be, My dwell - ing-place shall be. A - men.

2 COME, LET US SING OF A WONDERFUL LOVE

ROBERT WALMSLEY   ADAM WATSON

1. Come, let us sing of a won-der-ful love,   Ten - der and true,
2. Je - sus the Sa-viour this gos-pel to tell,   Joy - ful - ly came,
3. Je - sus is seek-ing the wan-der-ers yet;   Why do they roam?
4. Come to my heart, O thou won-der-ful love,   Come and a - bide,

ten - der and true;   Out of the heart of the Fa-ther a - bove,
joy - ful - ly came;   Came with the help - less and hope-less to dwell,
why do they roam?   Love on-ly waits to for - give and for - get;
come and a - bide;   Lift - ing my life till it ris - es a - bove

Stream-ing to me and to you: ___   Won-der - ful love,
Shar - ing their sor - row and shame: ___   Seek-ing the lost,
Home! wea - ry wan - der-ers, home! ___   Won-der - ful love,
En - vy and false-hood and pride: ___   Seek ing to be,

won-der-ful love   Dwells in the heart of the Fa-ther a - bove.
seek-ing the lost;   Sav - ing, re-deem-ing at meas-ure-less cost.
won-der-ful love   Dwells in the heart of the Fa-ther a - bove.
seek ing to be   Low - ly and hum-ble, a learn-er of Thee. A-men.

Words and Music by permission of J. Curwen & Sons, Ltd., London, Eng.

3 'TIS THE BLESSED HOUR OF PRAYER

Fanny J. Crosby

W. H. Doane

1. 'Tis the bless-ed hour of prayer, when our hearts low-ly bend,
2. 'Tis the bless-ed hour of prayer, when the Sav-ior draws near,
3. 'Tis the bless-ed hour of prayer, when the tempt-ed and tried
4. At the bless-ed hour of prayer, trust-ing Him, we be-lieve

And we gath-er to Je-sus, our Sav-ior and Friend;
With a ten-der com-pas-sion His chil-dren to hear;
To the Sav-ior who loves them their sor-row con-fide;
That the bless-ing we're need-ing we'll sure-ly re-ceive;

If we come to Him in faith, His pro-tec-tion to share,
When He tells us we may cast at His feet ev-'ry care,
With a sym-pa-thiz-ing heart He re-moves ev-'ry care;
In the full-ness of this trust we shall lose ev-'ry care;

CHORUS

What a balm for the wea-ry! O how sweet to be there! Bless-ed hour of prayer,

Bless-ed hour of prayer, What a balm for the wea-ry! O how sweet to be there!

4

FACE TO FACE

Mrs. Frank A. Breck
Moderato.

Grant Colfax Tullar

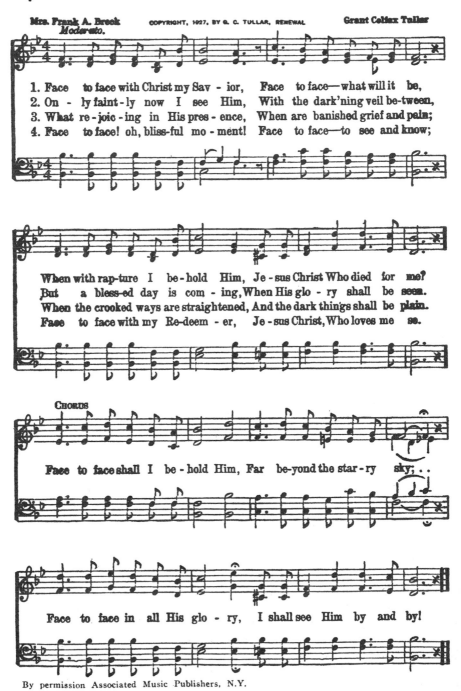

1. Face to face with Christ my Sav - ior, Face to face—what will it be,
2. On - ly faint-ly now I see Him, With the dark'ning veil be-tween,
3. What re-joic-ing in His pres - ence, When are banished grief and pain;
4. Face to face! oh, bliss-ful mo - ment! Face to face—to see and know;

When with rap-ture I be-hold Him, Je - sus Christ Who died for me?
But a bless-ed day is com - ing, When His glo - ry shall be seen.
When the crooked ways are straightened, And the dark things shall be plain.
Face to face with my Re-deem - er, Je - sus Christ, Who loves me so.

Chorus

Face to face shall I be-hold Him, Far be-yond the star - ry sky; . .

Face to face in all His glo - ry, I shall see Him by and by!

5

THE OLD RUGGED CROSS

REV. GEO. BENNARD

REV. GEO. BENNARD

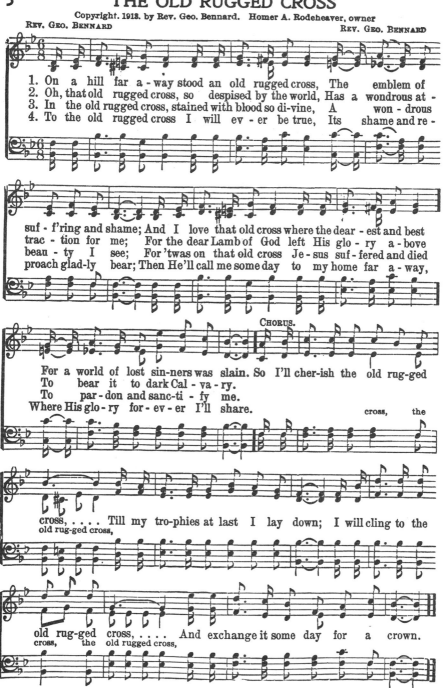

1. On a hill far a-way stood an old rugged cross, The emblem of
2. Oh, that old rugged cross, so despised by the world, Has a wondrous at -
3. In the old rugged cross, stained with blood so di-vine, A won - drous
4. To the old rugged cross I will ev - er be true, Its shame and re -

suf - f'ring and shame; And I love that old cross where the dear - est and best
trac - tion for me; For the dear Lamb of God left His glo - ry a - bove
beau - ty I see; For 'twas on that old cross Je - sus suf - fered and died
proach glad-ly bear; Then He'll call me some day to my home far a - way,

CHORUS.

For a world of lost sin-ners was slain. So I'll cher-ish the old rug-ged
To bear it to dark Cal - va - ry.
To par-don and sanc-ti - fy me.
Where His glo - ry for - ev - er I'll share.

cross, the

cross, ... Till my tro-phies at last I lay down; I will cling to the
old rug-ged cross,

old rug-ged cross, ... And exchange it some day for a crown.
cross,   the   old rugged cross,

6   SWEETER AS THE YEARS GO BY

Mrs. C. H. M.

Mrs. C. H. Morris

1. Of Je-sus' love that sought me, When I was lost in sin; Of won-drous
2. He trod in old Ju-de-a Life's pathway long a-go; The peo-ple
3. 'Twas wondrous love which led Him For us to suf-fer loss— To bear with-

grace that brought me Back to His fold a-gain; Of heights and depths of
thronged a-bout Him, His sav-ing grace to know; He healed the bro-ken
out a mur-mur, The an-guish of the cross; With saints redeemed in

mer - cy, Far deep-er than the sea, And high-er than the heaven's, My
heart-ed, And caused the blind to see; And still His great heart yearneth In
glo - ry, Let us our voic-es raise, Till heav'n and earth re-ech-o With

CHORUS

theme shall ev-er be.   Sweet-er as the years go by, ...
love for e-ven me.
our Redeemer's praise.   Sweet - er as the years go by, 'Tis

Sweet-er as the years go by;   Rich-er, full-er, deep-er,
sweet - er as the years go by;

SWEETER AS THE YEARS GO BY

Je - sus' love is sweet - er, Sweet - er as the years go by.

7 JESUS IS CALLING

Fanny J. Crosby

George C. Stebbins

1. Je - sus is ten-der-ly call-ing thee home—Call-ing to - day, call-ing to - day;
2. Je - sus is call-ing the wea - ry to rest— Call-ing to - day, call-ing to - day;
3. Je - sus is wait-ing, O come to Him now—Waiting to - day, wait-ing to - day;
4. Je - sus is pleading, O list to His voice—Hear Him to - day, hear Him to - day;

Why from the sun-shine of love wilt thou roam Far-ther and far-ther a - way?
Bring Him thy bur-den and thou shalt be blest; He will not turn thee a - way.
Come with thy sins, at His feet low - ly bow; Come, and no lon - ger de - lay.
They who be - lieve on His name shall re-joice; Quick-ly a - rise and a - way.

CHORUS

Call - - ing to - day! . . . Call - - ing to - day! . . .
Call - ing, call-ing to - day, to - day! Call - ing, call-ing to - day, to - day!

Je - - sus is call - - ing, Is ten-der-ly call-ing to - day.
Je - sus is ten-der - ly call-ing to-day,

THY WORD IS LIKE A GARDEN, LORD

EDWIN HODDER

Old English Melody

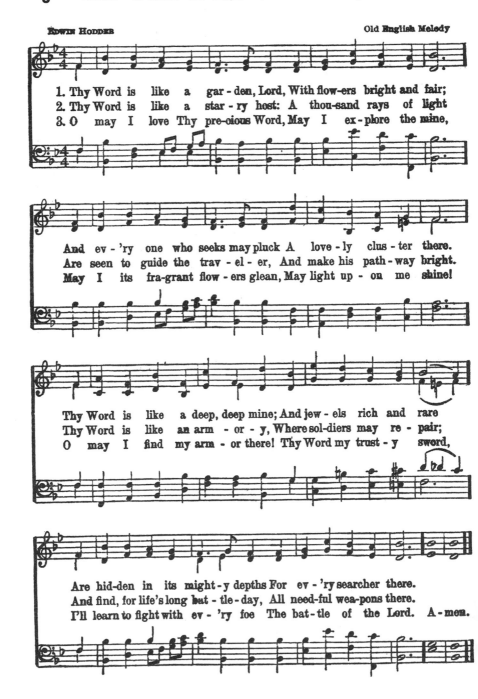

1. Thy Word is like a gar - den, Lord, With flow-ers bright and fair;
2. Thy Word is like a star - ry host: A thou-sand rays of light
3. O may I love Thy pre-cious Word, May I ex - plore the mine,

And ev - 'ry one who seeks may pluck A love - ly clus - ter there.
Are seen to guide the trav - el - er, And make his path - way bright.
May I its fra-grant flow - ers glean, May light up - on me shine!

Thy Word is like a deep, deep mine; And jew - els rich and rare
Thy Word is like an arm - or - y, Where sol-diers may re - pair;
O may I find my arm - or there! Thy Word my trust - y sword,

Are hid-den in its might - y depths For ev - 'ry searcher there.
And find, for life's long bat - tle - day, All need-ful wea-pons there.
I'll learn to fight with ev - 'ry foe The bat - tle of the Lord. A - men.

9

MY TASK

MAUDE LOUISE RAY

E. L. ASHFOOD

love some one more dear-ly ev-'ry day, To help a wan-d'ring child to find his
fol - low truth as blind men long for light, To do my best from dawn of day till

way, To pon-der o'er a no-ble thought, and pray, And smile when
night, To keep my heart fit for His ho - ly sight, And an - swer

eve-ning falls, And smile when eve-ning falls, This is my task.
when He calls, And an - swer when He calls, This is my task.

* The signs in brackets
are for 1st verse only.

Arrangement copyright **1942** by Gordon V. Thompson Limited, Toronto.

SINCE JESUS CAME INTO MY HEART

R. H. McDaniel

Chas. H. Gabriel

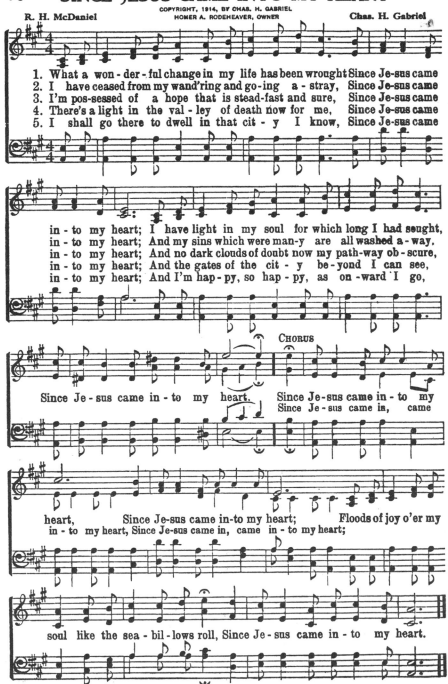

1. What a won-der-ful change in my life has been wrought Since Je-sus came
2. I have ceased from my wand'ring and go-ing a-stray, Since Je-sus came
3. I'm pos-sessed of a hope that is stead-fast and sure, Since Je-sus came
4. There's a light in the val-ley of death now for me, Since Je-sus came
5. I shall go there to dwell in that cit-y I know, Since Je-sus came

in-to my heart; I have light in my soul for which long I had sought,
in-to my heart; And my sins which were man-y are all washed a-way,
in-to my heart; And no dark clouds of doubt now my path-way ob-scure,
in-to my heart; And the gates of the cit-y be-yond I can see,
in-to my heart; And I'm hap-py, so hap-py, as on-ward I go,

Since Je-sus came in-to my heart.

CHORUS

Since Je-sus came in-to my
Since Je-sus came in, came

heart, Since Je-sus came in-to my heart; Floods of joy o'er my
in-to my heart, Since Je-sus came in, came in-to my heart;

soul like the sea-bil-lows roll, Since Je-sus came in-to my heart.

THE BEAUTIFUL GARDEN OF PRAYER

11

ELEANOR ALLEN SCHROLL   J. H. FILLMORE

1. There's a gar-den where Je-sus is wait-ing, There's a place that is
2. There's a gar-den where Je-sus is wait-ing, And I go with my
3. There's a gar-den where Je-sus is wait-ing, And He bids you to

won-drous-ly fair; For it glows with the light of His pres-ence, 'Tis the
bur-den and care, Just to learn from His lips words of com-fort, In the
come meet Him there; Just to bow and re-ceive a new bless-ing, In the

REFRAIN

beau-ti-ful gar-den of pray'r. O the beau-ti-ful gar-den, the

garden of pray'r, O the beau-ti-ful gar-den of pray'r; There my Savior a-

waits, and He o-pens the gates To the beau-ti-ful gar-den of pray'r.

THE CHURCH IN THE WILDWOOD

W. S. P.

Dr. Wm. S. Pitts

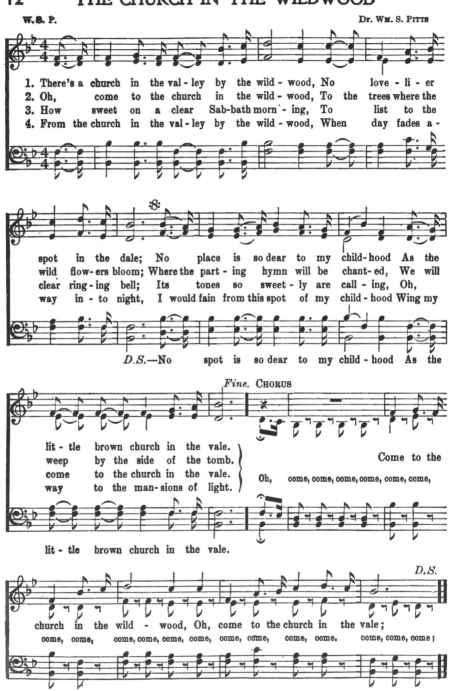

1. There's a church in the val-ley by the wild-wood, No love-li-er
2. Oh, come to the church in the wild-wood, To the trees where the
3. How sweet on a clear Sab-bath morn'-ing, To list to the
4. From the church in the val-ley by the wild-wood, When day fades a-

spot in the dale; No place is so dear to my child-hood As the
wild flow-ers bloom; Where the part-ing hymn will be chant-ed, We will
clear ring-ing bell; Its tones so sweet-ly are call-ing, Oh,
way in-to night, I would fain from this spot of my child-hood Wing my

D.S.—No spot is so dear to my child-hood As the

Fine. CHORUS

lit-tle brown church in the vale.
weep by the side of the tomb.
come to the church in the vale.
way to the man-sions of light.

Come to the

Oh, come, come, come, come, come, come, come,

lit-tle brown church in the vale.

D.S.

church in the wild-wood, Oh, come to the church in the vale;
come, come, come, come, come, come, come, come, come, come, come, come, come;

13 O MASTER, LET ME WALK WITH THEE

Washington Gladden

Robert Schumann

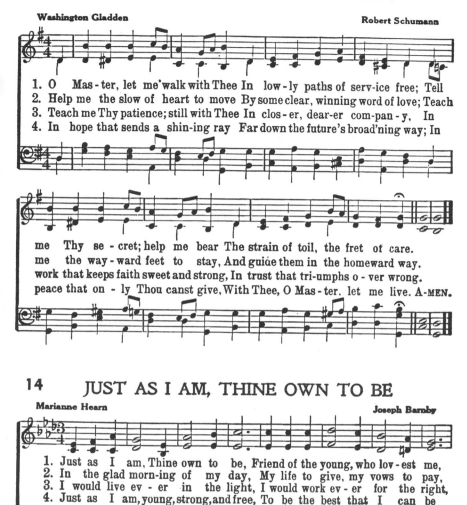

1. O Mas-ter, let me walk with Thee In low-ly paths of serv-ice free; Tell
2. Help me the slow of heart to move By some clear, winning word of love; Teach
3. Teach me Thy patience; still with Thee In clos-er, dear-er com-pan-y, In
4. In hope that sends a shin-ing ray Far down the future's broad'ning way; In

me Thy se-cret; help me bear The strain of toil, the fret of care.
me the way-ward feet to stay, And guide them in the homeward way.
work that keeps faith sweet and strong, In trust that tri-umphs o-ver wrong.
peace that on-ly Thou canst give, With Thee, O Mas-ter, let me live. A-MEN.

14 JUST AS I AM, THINE OWN TO BE

Marianne Hearn

Joseph Barnby

1. Just as I am, Thine own to be, Friend of the young, who lov-est me,
2. In the glad morn-ing of my day, My life to give, my vows to pay,
3. I would live ev-er in the light, I would work ev-er for the right,
4. Just as I am, young, strong, and free, To be the best that I can be

To con-se-crate my-self to Thee. O Je-sus Christ, I come.
With no re-serve and no de-lay, With all my heart I come.
I would serve Thee with all my might; There-fore, to Thee I come.
For truth, and right-eous-ness, and Thee, Lord of my life, I come.

15   THE STRANGER OF GALILEE

C. H. M.

Mrs. C. H. MORRIS

Moderately slow

In fan - cy I stood by the shore, one day, Of the beau - ti - ful murm'ring sea; ___ I
His look of com - pas-sion, His words of love, They shall nev - er for-got - ten be, ___ When
I heard Him speak peace to the an - gry waves, Of that tur - bu - lent, rag - ing sea; ___ And
Come ye who are driv-en, and tem - pest tossed, And His gra - cious sal - va - tion see; ___ He'll

saw the great crowds as they thronged the way Of the Stran - ger of Gal - i - lee; ___ I
sin - sick and help - less He saw me there This Stran - ger of Gal - i - lee; ___ He
lo! at His word are the wa - ters still'd, This Stran - ger of Gal - i - lee; ___ A
qui - et life's storms with His "Peace be still" This Stran - ger of Gal - i - lee; ___ He

saw how the man who was blind from birth, In a mo - ment was made to see; ___ The
showed me His hand and His riv - en side, And He whis - pered "It was for thee!" ___ My
peace - ful, a qui - et, and ho - ly calm Now and ev - er a - bides with me; ___ He
bids me to go and the sto - ry tell What He ev - er to you will be; ___ If

Arrangement copyright 1942 by Gordon V. Thompson Limited, Toronto

lame were made whole by the match - less skill Of the Stran - ger of Gal - i - lee. __
bur-den fell off at the pierc - ed feet Of the Stran-ger of Gal - i - lee. __
hold-eth my life in His might - y hands, This_ Stran-ger of Gal - i - lee. __
on - ly you let Him with you a - bide, This_ Stran-ger of Gal - i - lee. __

Chorus

And I felt I could love Him for - ev - er, So gra - cious and ten-der was
Oh my friend won't you love Him for - ev - er, So gra - cious and ten-der is

He! _____ I claim'd Him that day as my Sav - iour, This
He! _____ Ac - cept Him to day as your Sav - iour, This

Interlude

Stran-ger of Gal - i - lee. __
Stran-ger of Gal - i - lee. __

The Stranger Of Galilee - 2

BESIDE BLUE GALILEE

16

SOLO AND CHORUS

C. H. G.

Chas. H. Gabriel.

1. Be - side blue Gal - i - lee I stand Where once Thy footsteps marked the sand; I dream that Thou art with me, Lord—That I am list - 'ning to Thy word.
2. I look out o'er the rest-less sea, And muse and dream, my Lord, of Thee— O how the waves o - beyed Thy will, When Thou didst say to them, "Be still!"
3. And now ap-pears a hal-o'd wraith! It speaks! "O ye of lit - tle faith!" It is Thy form, Thy voice di-vine, That speaks to ev - 'ry heart, and mine!
4. Dear Mas - ter, hear my earn-est plea For grace, to walk up - on the sea; If such should be Thy wise be-hest, Oh, give me faith to stand the test!

CHORUS. (*First four measures from H. R. Palmer.*)

"O Gal - i - lee, blue Gal - i - lee, Gal - i - lee, ... Gal - i - lee,

Where Je - sus loved so much to be," Teach
Where Je - sus loved so much to be

rit.

me, O Lord, Thy ho - ly will, And whis-per to me, "Peace, be still!"

17 WHERE THE GATES SWING OUTWARD NEVER

C. H. G.

CHAS. H. GABRIEL

1. Just a few more days to be filled with praise, And to tell the
2. Just a few more years with their toil and tears, And the jour - ney
3. Tho' the hills be steep and the val - leys deep, With no flow'rs my
4. What a joy 'twill be when I wake to see Him for whom my

old, old sto - ry; Then, when twi - light falls, and my Sav - ior calls,
will be end - ed; Then I'll be with Him, where the tide of time
way a - dorn - ing; Tho' the night be lone and my rest a stone,
heart is burn - ing! Nev - er-more to sigh, nev - er-more to die—

CHORUS

I shall go to Him in glo - ry.
With e - ter - ni - ty is blend - ed. I'll exchange my cross for a
Joy a - waits me in the morn - ing.
For that day my heart is yearn - ing.

star - ry crown, Where the gates swing outward nev - er; At His feet I'll

lay ev - 'ry bur - den down, And with Je - sus reign for - ev - er.

18

TEACH ME, O LORD

MARTHA PUGH and G.V.T.

GORDON V. THOMPSON

1. Teach me, O Lord, to do What-e'er my hand may find; That
2. Teach me, O Lord, to give One-tenth of all I earn; And
3. Teach me, O Lord, to think And pon-der on Thy love; The
4. Teach me, O Lord, to live As ev-er in Thy sight; Teach

I may to my trust be true: Help me my sheaves to bind.
let me al-to-geth-er live That men of Thee may learn.
liv-ing wa-ter let me drink And point the way a-bove.
me the help-ing hand to give Or bat-tle for the right.

CHORUS

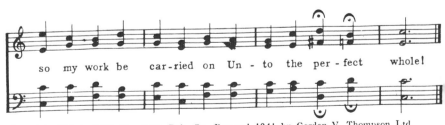

Then ere my task be done, Help me to touch some soul, That

so my work be car-ried on Un-to the per-fect whole!

19 FOLLOW THE GLEAM

Silver Bay Prize Song
BRYN MAWR COLLEGE

Sallie Hume Douglas

1. To the Knights in the days of old, Keep-ing watch on the
2. And we who would serve the King And loy - al - ly

moun - tain height, Came a vi - sion of Ho - ly Grail And a
Him o - bey, In the con - se-crate si - lence know That the

voice thro' the wait - ing night, Fol-low, fol - low, fol-low the gleam,
challenge still holds to - day. Fol-low, fol - low, fol-low the gleam,

REFRAIN

Ban - ners un-furled o'er all the world, Fol-low, fol - low,
Stand-ards of worth o'er all the earth, Fol-low, fol - low,

fol - low the gleam Of the Chal - ice that is the Grail.
fol - low the gleam Of the light that shall bring the dawn.

20 TELL ME THE STORY OF JESUS

Fanny J. Crosby

Jno. R. Sweney

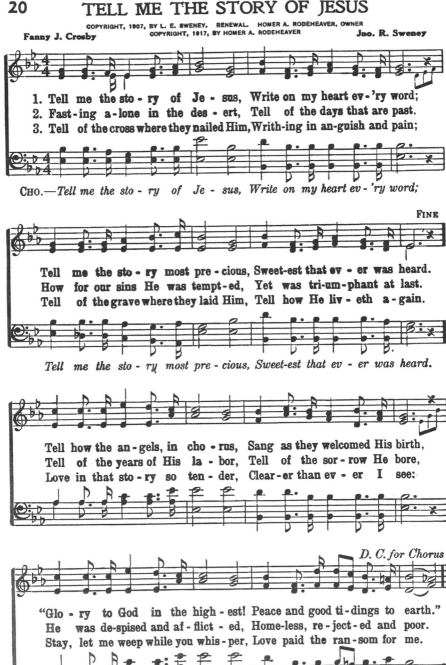

1. Tell me the sto - ry of Je - sus, Write on my heart ev - 'ry word;
2. Fast-ing a-lone in the des - ert, Tell of the days that are past,
3. Tell of the cross where they nailed Him, Writh-ing in an-guish and pain;

Cho.—*Tell me the sto - ry of Je - sus, Write on my heart ev - 'ry word;*

Tell me the sto - ry most pre - cious, Sweet-est that ev - er was heard.
How for our sins He was tempt-ed, Yet was tri-um-phant at last.
Tell of the grave where they laid Him, Tell how He liv - eth a - gain.

Tell me the sto - ry most pre - cious, Sweet-est that ev - er was heard.

Tell how the an - gels, in cho - rus, Sang as they welcomed His birth,
Tell of the years of His la - bor, Tell of the sor - row He bore,
Love in that sto - ry so ten - der, Clear-er than ev - er I see:

"Glo - ry to God in the high - est! Peace and good ti-dings to earth."
He was de-spised and af - flict - ed, Home-less, re - ject-ed and poor.
Stay, let me weep while you whis-per, Love paid the ran-som for me.

21 BRIGHTEN THE CORNER WHERE YOU ARE

INA DULEY OGDON

CHAS. H. GABRIEL

1. Do not wait un-til some deed of great-ness you may do, Do not
2. Just a-bove are cloud-ed skies that you may help to clear, Let not
3. Here for all your tal-ent you may sure-ly find a need, Here re-

wait to shed your light a-far, To the man-y du-ties ev-er near you
nar-row self your way de-bar, Tho' in-to one heart a-lone may fall your
flect the Bright and Morning Star, E-ven from your humble hand the bread of

now be true, Bright-en the cor-ner where you are.
song of cheer, Bright-en the cor-ner where you are. Bright-en the cor-ner
life may feed, Bright-en the cor-ner where you are.

REFRAIN

where you are! Bright-en the cor-ner where you are! Some one far from
Shine for Je-sus where you are!

har-bor you may guide a-cross the bar, Bright-en the cor-ner where you are.

22 MOTHER'S PRAYERS HAVE FOLLOWED ME

Lizzie DeArmond.   B. D. Ackley

1. I grieved my Lord from day to day, I scorned His love so full and
2. O'er des-ert wild, o'er mountain high A wan-der-er I chose to
3. He turned my dark-ness in-to light, This bless-ed Christ of Cal-va-

free, And though I wan-dered far a-way, My moth-er's
be, A wretch-ed soul con-demned to die, Still moth-er's
ry, I'll praise His name both day and night, That moth-er's

REFRAIN.

pray'rs have fol-lowed me. I'm com-ing home, I'm com-ing

home, To live my wast-ed life a-new, For moth-er's

pray'rs have fol-lowed me, Have fol-lowed me the whole world thro'.

IN THE GARDEN

C. A. M.

C. Austin Miles

1. I come to the gar-den a-lone, While the dew is still on the ros-es; And the voice I hear, Fall-ing on my ear; The Son of God dis-clos-es.

2. He speaks, and the sound of His voice Is so sweet the birds hush their sing-ing, And the mel-o-dy That He gave to me, With-in my heart is ring-ing.

3. I'd stay in the gar-den with Him Tho' the night a-round me be fall-ing, But He bids me go; Thro' the voice of woe, His voice to me is call-ing.

CHORUS

And He walks with me, and He talks with me, And He tells me I am His own, And the joy we share as we tar-ry there, None other has ev-er known.

24 AT THE CROSS

Isaac Watts

R. E. Hudson

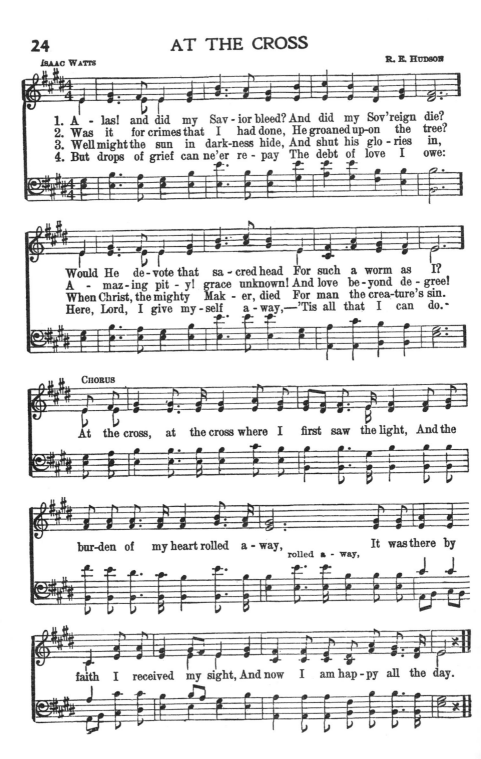

1. A - las! and did my Sav - ior bleed? And did my Sov'reign die?
2. Was it for crimes that I had done, He groaned up-on the tree?
3. Well might the sun in dark-ness hide, And shut his glo - ries in,
4. But drops of grief can ne'er re - pay The debt of love I owe:

Would He de-vote that sa - cred head For such a worm as I?
A - maz-ing pit - y! grace unknown! And love be-yond de - gree!
When Christ, the mighty Mak - er, died For man the crea-ture's sin.
Here, Lord, I give my-self a - way,—'Tis all that I can do.

Chorus

At the cross, at the cross where I first saw the light, And the
bur-den of my heart rolled a - way, rolled a - way,
It was there by
faith I received my sight, And now I am hap-py all the day.

25

LOVE LIFTED ME

COPYRIGHT, 1912, BY CHARLIE D. TILLMAN
ROBERT H. COLEMAN, OWNER

James Rowe

Howard E. Smith

1. I was sink-ing deep in sin, Far from the peaceful shore, Ver - y deep-ly
2. All my heart to Him I give, Ev - er to Him I'll cling, In His bless-ed
3. Souls in dan-ger, look a-bove, Je - sus com-plete-ly saves; He will lift you

stained with-in, Sink-ing to rise no more; But the Mas - ter of the sea
pres - ence live, Ev - er His prais-es sing. Love so might-y and so true
by His love Out of the an - gry waves. He's the Mas-ter of the sea,

Heard my de-spair-ing cry, From the wa-ters lift - ed me, Now safe am I.
Mer - its my soul's best songs; Faith-ful, lov-ing serv-ice, too, To Him be - longs.
Bil - lows His will o - bey; He your Sav-ior wants to be—Be saved to - day.

CHORUS

Love lift - ed me! . . . . Love lift - ed me! . . . . When noth - ing
e - ven me!   e - ven me!

else could help, Love lift - ed me.   Love lift - ed me.   A - MEN.

WHEN THE ROLL IS CALLED UP YONDER

J. M. B.

J. M. Black

1. When the trumpet of the Lord shall sound, and time shall be no more, And the
2. On that bright and cloudless morning when the dead in Christ shall rise, And the
3. Let us la - bor for the Mas - ter from the dawn till set - ting sun, Let us

morning breaks, e-ter-nal, bright and fair; When the saved of earth shall gather
glo - ry of His res - ur-rec-tion share; When His cho-sen ones shall gather
talk of all His wondrous love and care; Then when all of life is o - ver,

o - ver on the oth-er shore, And the roll is called up yon-der, I'll be there.
to their home beyond the skies, And the roll is called up yon-der, I'll be there.
and our work on earth is done, And the roll is called up yon-der, I'll be there.

CHORUS.

When the roll . . . . . . is called up yon - - - - der, When the
When the roll is called up yon-der, I'll be there,

roll . . . . is called up yon - - der, When the roll . . . . is called up
When the roll is called up yon-der, I'll be there, When the roll is called up

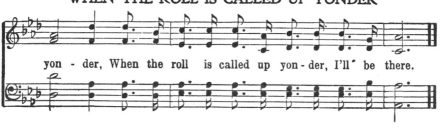

yon - der, When the roll is called up yon - der, I'll be there.

21

WHAT A FRIEND

JOSEPH SCRIVEN

CHARLES C. CONVERSE

1. What a Friend we have in Je - sus, All our sins and griefs to bear!
2. Have we tri - als and temp - ta - tions? Is there trou-ble an - y-where?
3. Are we weak and heav-y - la - den, Cumbered with a load of care?—

What a priv - i - lege to car - ry Ev - 'ry-thing to God in pray'r!
We should nev - er be dis - cour - aged, Take it to 'the Lord in pray'r.
Pre - cious Sav-ior, still our ref - uge,—Take it to the Lord in pray'r.

O what peace we oft - en for - feit, O what needless pain we bear,
Can we find a friend so faith - ful Who will all our sor-rows share?
Do thy friends despise, for-sake thee? Take it to the Lord in pray'r;

All because we do not car - ry Ev - 'ry-thing to God in pray'r!
Je - sus knows our ev - 'ry weak - ness, Take it to the Lord in pray'r.
In His arms He'll take and shield thee, Thou wilt find a sol - ace there.

28 YOU MAY HAVE THE JOYBELLS

J. Edw. Ruark

Wm. J. Kirkpatrick

1. You may have the joy-bells ring-ing in your heart, And a peace that
2. Love of Je-sus in its full-ness you may know, And this love to
3. You will meet with tri-als as you jour-ney home, Grace suf-fi-cient
4. Let your life speak well of Je-sus ev-'ry day, Own His right to

from you nev-er will de-part; Walk the straight and nar-row way, Live for
those a-round you sweet-ly show; Words of kind-ness al-ways say, Deeds of
He will give to o-ver-come; Tho' un-seen by mor-tal eye, He is
ev-'ry serv-ice you can pay; Sin-ners you can help to win If your

Je-sus ev-'ry day, He will keep the joy-bells ring-ing in your heart.
mer-cy do each day, Then He'll keep the joy-bells ring-ing in your heart.
with you ev-er nigh, And He'll keep the joy-bells ring-ing in your heart.
life is pure and clean, And you keep the joy-bells ring-ing in your heart.

D.S. He will keep the joy-bells ring-ing in your heart.

CHORUS

Joy - bells ring-ing in your heart, Joy - bells ring-ing
Ring-ing in your heart, You may have the joy-bells

in your heart; Take the Sav-ior here be-low, With you ev-'ry-where you go,

PRAISE HIM! PRAISE HIM!

FANNY J. CROSBY

CHESTER G. ALLEN

1. Praise Him! praise Him! Je-sus, our bless-ed Re-deem-er! Sing, O Earth, His
2. Praise Him! praise Him! Je-sus, our bless-ed Re-deem-er! For our sins He
3. Praise Him! praise Him! Je-sus, our bless-ed Re-deem-er! Heav'nly por-tals

won-der-ful love pro-claim! Hail Him! hail Him! highest archangels in glo-ry;
suffered, and bled, and died; He our Rock, our hope of e-ter-nal sal-va-tion,
loud with ho-san-nas ring! Je-sus, Sav-ior, reigneth for-ev-er and ev-er;

Strength and hon-or give to His ho-ly name! Like a shep-herd, Je-sus will
Hail Him! hail Him! Je-sus the Cru-ci-fied. Sound His Praises! Je-sus who
Crown Him! crown Him! Prophet, and Priest, and King! Christ is com-ing! o-ver the

REFRAIN

guard His children, In His arms He carries them all day long:
bore our sorrows, Love unbounded, wonderful, deep and strong: Praise Him! praise Him!
world vic-to-rious, Pow'r and glo-ry un-to the Lord be-long:

tell of His ex-cel-lent greatness; Praise Him! praise Him! ev-er in joy-ful song!

FANNY J. CROSBY

JNO. R. SWENEY

1. When my life-work is end-ed, and I cross the swell-ing tide, When the
2. Oh, the soul-thrill-ing rap-ture when I view His bless-ed face, And the
3. Oh, the dear ones in glo-ry, how they beck-on me to come, And our
4. Thro' the gates to the cit-y in a robe of spot-less white, He will

bright and glorious morning I shall see; I shall know my Re-deem-er when I
lus-ter of His kind-ly beaming eye; How my full heart will praise Him for the
part-ing at the riv-er I re-call; To the sweet vales of E-den they will
lead me where no tears will ev-er fall; In the glad song of a-ges I shall

reach the oth-er side, And His smile will be the first to wel-come me.
mer-cy, love, and grace, That pre-pare for me a man-sion in the sky.
sing my wel-come home; But I long to meet my Sav-ior first of all.
min-gle with de-light; But I long to meet my Sav-ior first of all.

CHORUS

I shall know . . Him, I shall know Him, And redeemed by His side I shall stand,
I shall know Him,

I shall know . . Him, I shall know Him By the print of the nails in His hand.
I shall know Him,

31 SAIL ON!

C. H. G.

COPYRIGHT, 1937, RENEWAL
THE RODEHEAVER CO., OWNER

Chas. H. Gabriel.

Solo and chorus.

1. Up-on a wide and stormy sea, Thou'rt sail-ing to e-ter-ni-ty,
2. Art far from shore, and wea-ry-worn—The sky o'er-cast, the can-vas torn?
3. Do comrades trem-ble and re-fuse To fur-ther dare the taunting hues?
4. Do snarling waves thy craft as-sail? Art pow'rless, drift-ing with the gale?

Ad lib.

And thy great Ad-m'ral or-ders Thee:—"Sail on! sail on! sail on!"
Hark ye! a voice to thee is borne:—"Sail on! sail on! sail on!"
No oth-er course is thine to choose, Sail on! sail on! sail on!
Take heart! God's word shall nev-er fail! Sail on! sail on! sail on!

CHORUS.

Sail on! sail on! the storms will soon be past, The dark-ness

will not al-ways last; Sail on! sail on!...... God

Sail on! sail on!

* Rit. e dim *pp*

lives! and He commands:"Sail on! sail on!"......

on! sail on! sail on sail on!

32

LORD, IS IT I?

G. V. T.

GORDON V. THOMPSON

1. Some-one is slight-ing the Sav-ior to-day, Nev-er once heed-ing what He has to say. Some-one is drift-ing still far-ther a-way— Tell me, O Lord, is it I?
2. Some-one's neg-lect-ing the poor in their need, Some hun-gry soul he could eas-i-ly feed. Some-one is fail-ing to sow pre-cious seed— Tell me, O Lord, is it I?
3. Some-one is walk-ing with Je-sus to-day, Scat-ter-ing sun-shine o'er life's dark-ened way; Some-one will live through an un-end-ing day— Tell me, O Lord, is it I?

CHORUS

Lord, ___ is it I? ___ Tell me, Lord, ___ is it I? ___ Can it pos-si-bly be That my Sav-ior means

Lord, is it I? Lord, is it I? Lord, is it I? Tell me Lord, is it I?

me? Lord, _____ is it I? _____
Bless-ed Lord, is it I?   Lord, is it I?

33 IN HEAVENLY LOVE ABIDING

ANNA L. WARING   SAMUEL S. WESLEY

1. In heav-'nly love a - bid - ing, No change my heart shall fear; And
2. Wher - ev - er He may guide me, No want shall turn me back; My
3. Green pas-tures are be - fore me, Which yet I have not seen; Bright

safe is such con - fid - ing, For noth-ing chang-es here: The
Shep-herd is be - side me, And noth-ing can I lack: His
skies will soon be o'er me, Where dark-est clouds have been: My

storm may roar with - out me, My heart may low be laid, But
wis - dom ev - er wak-eth; His sight is nev - er dim; He
hope I can-not meas-ure, My path to life is free, My

God is round a - bout me, And can I be dis - mayed?
knows the way He tak - eth, And I will walk with Him.
Sav - ior has my treas-ure, And He will walk with me.

34 TRUE-HEARTED, WHOLE-HEARTED

Frances R. Havergal

George C. Stebbins

1. True-hearted, whole-hearted, faith-ful and loy-al, King of our lives, by Thy grace we will be; Un-der the stan-dard ex-alt-ed and roy-al, Strong in Thy strength we will bat-tle for Thee.

2. True-hearted, whole-hearted, full-est al-le-giance, Yielding henceforth to our glo-ri-ous King; Val-iant en-deav-or and lov-ing o-be-dience Free-ly and joy-ous-ly now we would bring.

3. True-hearted, whole-hearted, Sav-ior all-glo-rious! Take Thy great pow-er and reign there a-lone, O-ver our wills and af-fec-tions vic-to-rious, Free-ly sur-ren-dered and whol-ly Thine own.

CHORUS

Peal out the watchword! si-lence it nev-er, Song of our spir-its re-joic-ing and free; Peal out the watch-word! loy-al for-ev-er, King of our lives, by Thy grace we will be.

35   WE HAVE AN ANCHOR

Priscilla J. Owens   Wm. J. Kirkpatrick

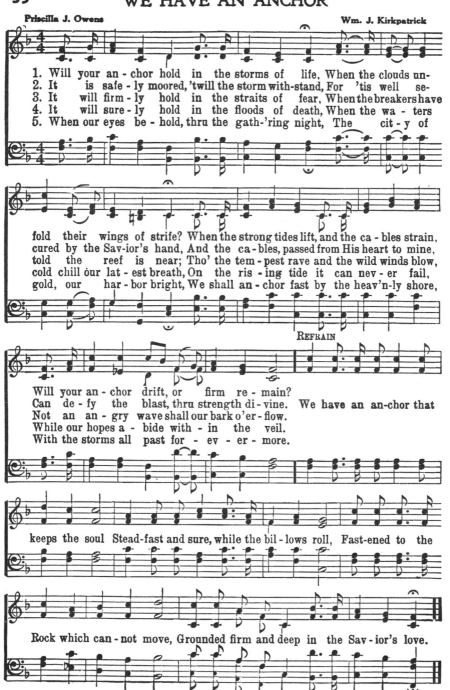

1. Will your an-chor hold in the storms of life, When the clouds un-
2. It is safe-ly moored, 'twill the storm with-stand, For 'tis well se-
3. It will firm-ly hold in the straits of fear, When the breakers have
4. It will sure-ly hold in the floods of death, When the wa-ters
5. When our eyes be-hold, thru the gath-'ring night, The cit-y of

fold their wings of strife? When the strong tides lift, and the ca-bles strain,
cured by the Sav-ior's hand, And the ca-bles, passed from His heart to mine,
told the reef is near; Tho' the tem-pest rave and the wild winds blow,
cold chill our lat-est breath, On the ris-ing tide it can nev-er fail,
gold, our har-bor bright, We shall an-chor fast by the heav'n-ly shore,

REFRAIN

Will your an-chor drift, or firm re-main?
Can de-fy the blast, thru strength di-vine. We have an an-chor that
Not an an-gry wave shall our bark o'er-flow.
While our hopes a-bide with-in the veil.
With the storms all past for-ev-er-more.

keeps the soul Stead-fast and sure, while the bil-lows roll, Fast-ened to the

Rock which can-not move, Grounded firm and deep in the Sav-ior's love.

O BEULAH LAND

EDGAR PAGE

JNO. R. SWENEY

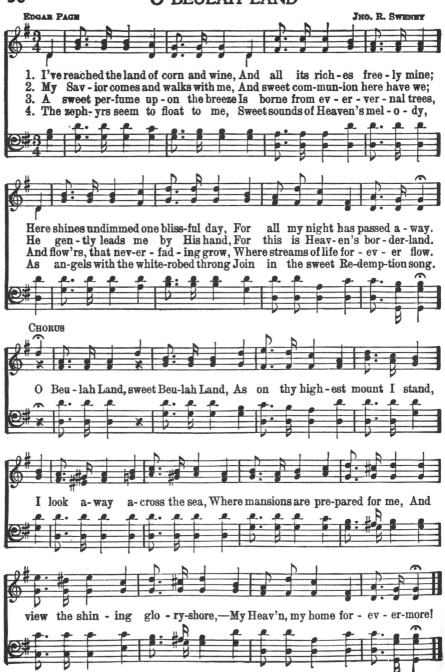

1. I've reached the land of corn and wine, And all its rich-es free-ly mine;
2. My Sav-ior comes and walks with me, And sweet com-mun-ion here have we;
3. A sweet per-fume up-on the breeze Is borne from ev-er-ver-nal trees,
4. The zeph-yrs seem to float to me, Sweet sounds of Heaven's mel-o-dy,

Here shines undimmed one bliss-ful day, For all my night has passed a-way.
He gen-tly leads me by His hand, For this is Heav-en's bor-der-land.
And flow'rs, that nev-er-fad-ing grow, Where streams of life for-ev-er flow.
As an-gels with the white-robed throng Join in the sweet Re-demp-tion song.

CHORUS

O Beu-lah Land, sweet Beu-lah Land, As on thy high-est mount I stand,

I look a-way a-cross the sea, Where mansions are pre-pared for me, And

view the shin-ing glo-ry-shore,—My Heav'n, my home for-ev-er-more!

WE'RE MARCHING TO ZION

ISAAC WATTS

ROBERT LOWRY

Spirited

1. Come, we that love the Lord, And let our joys be known, Join
2. Let those re - fuse to sing Who nev - er knew our God; But
3. The hill of Zi - on yields A thou - sand sa - cred sweets Be -
4. Then let our songs abound, And ev - 'ry tear be dry; We're

in a song with sweet ac - cord, Join in a song with sweet accord, And
chil - dren of the heav'n-ly King, But chil - dren of the heav'nly King, May
fore we reach the heav'n-ly fields, Be-fore we reach the heav'nly fields, Or
marching thro' Immanuel's ground, We're marching thro' Immanuel's ground, To

thus sur - round the throne, And thus sur-round the throne.
speak their joys a - broad, May speak their joys a - broad.
walk the gold - en streets, Or walk the gold - en streets.
fair - er worlds on high, To fair - er worlds on high.

thus sur - round the throne, And thus sur - round the throne.

CHORUS

We're march - ing to Zi - on, Beau-ti - ful, beau-ti-ful Zi - on; We're
We're marching on to Zi - on,

march-ing upward to Zi - on, The beau - ti-ful cit - y of God.
Zi - on, Zi - on,

SOUND THE BATTLE CRY

W. F. S.

WM. F. SHERWIN

1. Sound the bat - tle cry! See, the foe is nigh; Raise the standard high
2. Strong to meet the foe, Marching on we go, While our cause we know,
3. O! Thou God of all, Hear us when we call, Help us one and all

For the Lord; Gird your ar - mor on, Stand firm, ev - 'ry one; Rest your
Must pre-vail; Shield and banner bright, Gleam-ing in the light; Bat-tling
By Thy grace; When the bat-tle's done, And the vic-t'ry's won, May we

CHORUS ff

cause up - on His ho - ly word.
for the right We ne'er can fail. Rouse, then, sol - diers, ral - ly round the
wear the crown Be - fore Thy face.

ban - ner, Read - y, stead - y, pass the word a-long; On-ward, for-ward,

shout a - loud Ho - san - na! Christ is Cap - tain of the might - y throng.

39 THERE SHALL BE SHOWERS OF BLESSING

EL NATHAN   J. McGRANAHAN

1. There shall be show-ers of bless - ing: This is the promise of love;
2. There shall be show-ers of bless - ing— Pre-cious re - vi-ving a - gain;
3. There shall be show-ers of bless - ing: Send them up-on us, O Lord!
4. There shall be show-ers of bless - ing: O that to - day they might fall,
5. There shall be show-ers of bless - ing, If we but trust and o - bey;

There shall be sea-sons re - fresh - ing, Sent from the Sav-iour a - bove.
O - ver the hills and the val - leys, Sound of a-bun-dance of rain.
Grant to us now a re - fresh - ing; Come, and now hon-or Thy Word.
Now as to God we're con - fess - ing, Now as on Je - sus we call!
There shall be sea-sons re - fresh - ing, If we let God have His way.

CHORUS

Show - ers of bless - ing, Show-ers of bless-ing we need;
Show - ers, show-ers

Mer-cy-drops round us are fall - ing, But for the show-ers we plead.

STAND UP FOR JESUS

G. DUFFIELD

G. J. WEBB

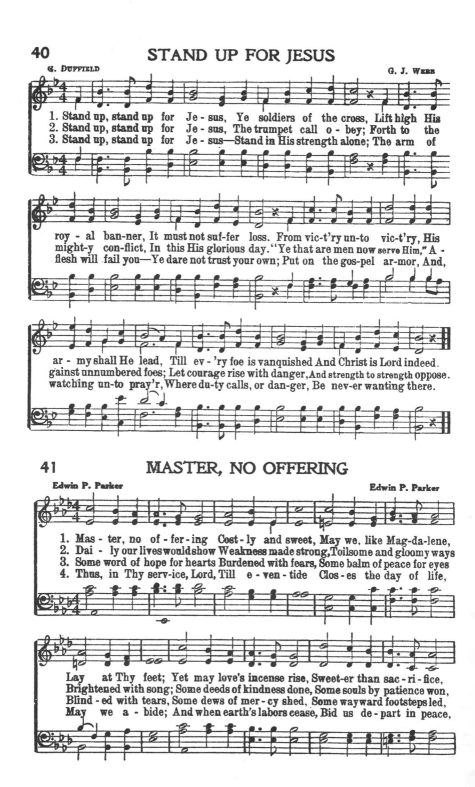

1. Stand up, stand up for Je - sus, Ye soldiers of the cross, Lift high His
2. Stand up, stand up for Je - sus, The trumpet call o - bey; Forth to the
3. Stand up, stand up for Je - sus—Stand in His strength alone; The arm of

roy - al ban-ner, It must not suf-fer loss. From vic-t'ry un-to vic-t'ry, His
might-y con-flict, In this His glorious day."Ye that are men now serve Him," A -
flesh will fail you—Ye dare not trust your own; Put on the gos-pel ar-mor, And,

ar - my shall He lead, Till ev - 'ry foe is vanquished And Christ is Lord indeed.
gainst unnumbered foes; Let courage rise with danger,And strength to strength oppose.
watching un-to pray'r,Where du-ty calls, or dan-ger, Be nev-er wanting there.

41 MASTER, NO OFFERING

Edwin P. Parker

Edwin P. Parker

1. Mas - ter, no of - fer-ing Cost-ly and sweet, May we, like Mag-da-lene,
2. Dai - ly our lives would show Weakness made strong,Toilsome and gloomy ways
3. Some word of hope for hearts Burdened with fears, Some balm of peace for eyes
4. Thus, in Thy serv-ice, Lord, Till e - ven - tide Clos-es the day of life,

Lay at Thy feet; Yet may love's incense rise, Sweet-er than sac - ri - fice,
Brightened with song; Some deeds of kindness done, Some souls by patience won,
Blind - ed with tears, Some dews of mer - cy shed, Some wayward footsteps led,
May we a - bide; And when earth's labors cease, Bid us de - part in peace,

MASTER, NO OFFERING

Dear   Lord,   to   Thee. . . . Dear Lord,   to   Thee.   A - MEN.

42   LET THE LOWER LIGHTS BE BURNING

P. P. B.   Used by permission   P. P. BLISS

1. Bright-ly beams our Fa-ther's mer-cy From His lighthouse ev - er - more;
2. Dark the night of sin has set-tled, Loud the an - gry bil-lows roar;
3. Trim your fee - ble lamp, my brother! Some poor sea - man, tempest-tossed,

But   to   us   He gives the keep-ing   Of   the lights a - long the shore.
Ea - ger eyes   are watching, long-ing,   For   the lights a - long the shore.
Try - ing now   to make the har-bor,   In   the dark-ness may   be   lost.

CHORUS

Let   the low - er lights be burning! Send   a gleam   a-cross   the wave!

Some poor fainting, struggling sea-man You   may res - cue, you   may save.

CROWN HIM WITH MANY CROWNS

MATTHEW BRIDGES   GEORGE J. ELVEY

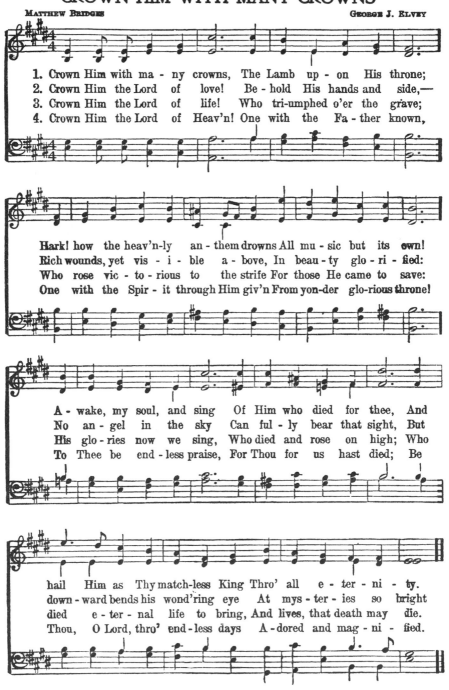

1. Crown Him with ma - ny crowns, The Lamb up - on His throne;
2. Crown Him the Lord of love! Be - hold His hands and side,—
3. Crown Him the Lord of life! Who tri-umphed o'er the grave;
4. Crown Him the Lord of Heav'n! One with the Fa - ther known,

Hark! how the heav'n-ly an - them drowns All mu - sic but its own!
Rich wounds, yet vis - i - ble a - bove, In beau - ty glo - ri - fied:
Who rose vic - to - rious to the strife For those He came to save:
One with the Spir - it through Him giv'n From yon-der glo-rious throne!

A - wake, my soul, and sing Of Him who died for thee, And
No an - gel in the sky Can ful - ly bear that sight, But
His glo - ries now we sing, Who died and rose on high; Who
To Thee be end - less praise, For Thou for us hast died; Be

hail Him as Thy match-less King Thro' all e - ter - ni - ty.
down - ward bends his wond'ring eye At mys - ter - ies so bright
died e - ter - nal life to bring, And lives, that death may die.
Thou, O Lord, thro' end - less days A - dored and mag - ni - fied.

44 RING THE BELLS OF HEAVEN

Rev. W. O. Cushing
Joyfully

G. F. Root

1. Ring the bells of heav-en! there is joy to-day, For a soul re-
2. Ring the bells of heav-en! there is joy to-day, For the wan-d'rer
3. Ring the bells of heav-en! spread the feast to-day! An-gels, swell the

turn-ing from the wild! See! the Fa-ther meets him out up-on the way,
now is rec-on-ciled; Yes, a soul is res-cued from his sin-ful way,
glad tri-um-phant strain! Tell the joy-ful ti-dings, bear it far a-way!

CHORUS

Wel-com-ing His wea-ry, wan-d'ring child.
And is born a-new a ran-somed child. Glo-ry! glo-ry! how the
For a pre-cious soul is born a-gain.

an-gels sing; Glo-ry! glo-ry! how the loud harps ring! 'Tis the ran-somed

ar-my, like a might-y sea, Peal-ing forth the an-them of the free.

45   YIELD NOT TO TEMPTATION

H. R. P.

Dr. H. R. PALMER

1. Yield not to temp-ta-tion, For yield-ing is sin; Each vic-t'ry will help you Some oth-er to win; Fight man-ful-ly on-ward, Dark pas-sions sub-due; Look ev-er to Je-sus, He'll car-ry you through.

2. Shun e-vil com-pan-ions, Bad lan-guage dis-dain; God's name hold in rev-'rence, Nor take it in vain; Be thought-ful and ear-nest, Kind-heart-ed 'and true; Look ev-er to Je-sus, He'll car-ry you through.

3. To him that o'er-com-eth, God giv-eth a crown; Thro' faith we will con-quer, Tho' oft-en cast down; He who is our Sav-ior, Our strength will re-new; Look ev-er to Je-sus, He'll car-ry you through.

CHORUS

Ask the Sav-ior to help you, Com-fort, strength-en, and keep you; He is will-ing to aid you, He will car-ry you through.

46 STANDING ON THE PROMISES

R. K. C.

B. KELSO CARTER

1. Stand-ing on the prom-is-es of Christ my King, Thro' e-ter-nal
2. Stand-ing on the prom-is-es that can-not fail, When the howl-ing
3. Stand-ing on the prom-is-es I now can see Per-fect, pres-ent
4. Stand-ing on the prom-is-es of Christ the Lord, Bound to Him e-
5. Stand-ing on the prom-is-es I can-not fall, List'ning ev-'ry

a-ges let His prais-es ring; Glo-ry in the highest I will shout and sing,
storms of doubt and fear as-sail, By the liv-ing Word of God I shall pre-vail,
cleansing in the blood for me; Standing in the lib-erty where Christ makes free,
ter-nal-ly by love's strong cord, O-ver-com-ing dai-ly with the Spir-it's sword,
mo-ment to the Spir-it's call, Rest-ing in my Sav-ior, as my all in all,

Chorus

Standing on the promis-es of God. Stand-ing, stand-ing,
Standing on the promises, Standing on the promises,

Stand-ing on the promis-es of God my Sav-ior; Stand-ing,
Standing on the prom-is-es,

stand-ing, I'm stand-ing on the prom-is-es of God.
Stand-ing on the prom-is-es,

47

SUNLIGHT

J. W. Van De Venter

W. S. Weeden

1. I wan-dered in the shades of night, Till Je - sus came to me,
2. Tho' clouds may gath-er in the sky, And bil - lows round me roll,
3. While walk - ing in the light of God, I sweet com-mun - ion find;
4. I cross the wide ex - tend - ed fields, I jour-ney o'er the plain,
5. Soon I shall see him as he is, The Light that came to me;

And with the sun-light of his love Bid all my dark-ness flee.
How - ev - er dark the world may be I've sun-light in my soul.
I press with ho - ly vig - or on And leave the world be - hind.
And in the sun-light of his love I reap the gold-en grain.
Be - hold the brightness of his face, Through-out e - ter - ni - ty.

CHORUS

Sun-light, sun-light, in my soul to-day, Sun - light, sun - light
to-day, yes,

all a - long the way, Since the Sav-iour found me,
nar - row way,

load of sin,
took a-way my sin, I have had the sun-light of his love with-in.

48 WE'VE A STORY TO TELL TO THE NATIONS

COLIN STERNE   Used by permission of the composer   H. ERNEST NICHOL

1. We've a sto-ry to tell to the na-tions That shall turn their hearts
2. We've a song to be sung to the na-tions That shall lift their hearts
3. We've a mes-sage to give to the na-tions, That the Lord who reign-
4. We've a Sav-ior to show to the na-tions Who the path of sor-

1. That shall turn

to the right,   A sto-ry of truth and mer-cy,   A
to the Lord,   A song that shall con-quer e-vil   And
eth a-bove   Hath sent us His Son to save us,   And
row hath trod,   That all of the world's great peo-ples   Might

their hearts to the right,

sto-ry of peace and light, A sto-ry of peace and light.
shat-ter the spear and sword, And shat-ter the spear and sword.
show us that God is love, And show us that God is love.
come to the truth of God, Might come to the truth of God.

A sto - ry of peace and light.

CHORUS

For the darkness shall turn to dawn-ing, And the dawning to noonday bright,

rall.

And Christ's great kingdom shall come to earth, The kingdom of love and light.

49 THROW OUT THE LIFE-LINE

E. S. Ufford

E. S. Ufford. Arr. by Geo. C. Stebbins

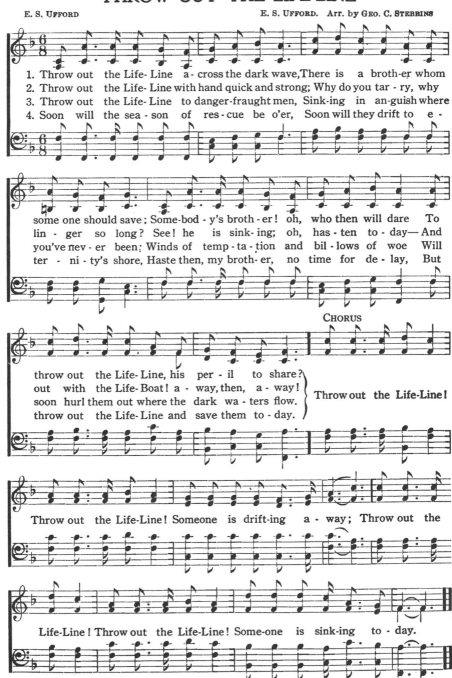

1. Throw out the Life-Line a-cross the dark wave, There is a broth-er whom some one should save; Some-bod-y's broth-er! oh, who then will dare To throw out the Life-Line, his per-il to share?

2. Throw out the Life-Line with hand quick and strong; Why do you tar-ry, why lin-ger so long? See! he is sink-ing; oh, has-ten to-day— And out with the Life-Boat! a-way, then, a-way!

3. Throw out the Life-Line to danger-fraught men, Sink-ing in an-guish where you've nev-er been; Winds of temp-ta-tion and bil-lows of woe Will soon hurl them out where the dark wa-ters flow.

4. Soon will the sea-son of res-cue be o'er, Soon will they drift to e-ter-ni-ty's shore, Haste then, my broth-er, no time for de-lay, But throw out the Life-Line and save them to-day.

CHORUS

Throw out the Life-Line! Throw out the Life-Line! Someone is drift-ing a-way; Throw out the Life-Line! Throw out the Life-Line! Some-one is sink-ing to-day.

50 THE WAY OF THE CROSS LEADS HOME

JESSIE BROWN POUNDS COPYRIGHT, 1934. RENEWAL.   HOMER A. RODEHEAVER, OWNER CHAS. H. GABRIEL

1. I must needs go home by the way of the cross, There's no oth-er way but this; I shall ne'er get sight of the Gates of Light, If the way of the cross I miss.

2. I must needs go on in the blood-sprinkled way, The path that the Sav-ior trod, If I ev-er climb to the heights sub-lime, Where the soul is at home with God.

3. Then I bid fare-well to the way of the world, To walk in it nev-er-more; For my Lord says "Come," and I seek my home, Where He waits at the o-pen door.

CHORUS.

The way of the cross leads home, The way of the cross leads home; It is sweet to know, as I on-ward go, The way of the cross leads home. A-MEN.

(leads home, leads home;)

GLORIOUS THINGS OF THEE ARE SPOKEN

John Newton

Francis J. Haydn

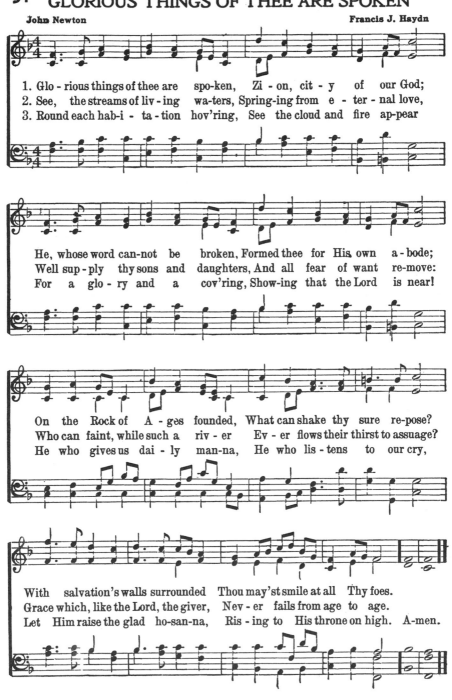

1. Glo - rious things of thee are spo-ken, Zi - on, cit - y of our God;
2. See, the streams of liv - ing wa-ters, Spring-ing from e - ter - nal love,
3. Round each hab-i - ta - tion hov'ring, See the cloud and fire ap-pear

He, whose word can-not be broken, Formed thee for His own a - bode;
Well sup - ply thy sons and daughters, And all fear of want re-move:
For a glo - ry and a cov'ring, Show-ing that the Lord is near!

On the Rock of A - ges founded, What can shake thy sure re-pose?
Who can faint, while such a riv - er Ev - er flows their thirst to assuage?
He who gives us dai - ly man-na, He who lis - tens to our cry,

With salvation's walls surrounded Thou may'st smile at all Thy foes.
Grace which, like the Lord, the giver, Nev - er fails from age to age.
Let Him raise the glad ho-san-na, Ris - ing to His throne on high. A-men.

52 BRINGING IN THE SHEAVES

Knowles Shaw

George A. Minor

1. Sow-ing in the morn-ing, sow-ing seeds of kind-ness, Sow-ing in the
2. Sow-ing in the sun-shine, sow-ing in the shad-ows, Fear-ing nei-ther
3. Go-ing forth with weep-ing, sow-ing for the Mas-ter, Tho' the loss sus-

noon-tide and the dew-y eve; Wait-ing for the har-vest,
clouds nor win-ter's chill-ing breeze; By and by the har-vest,
tained our spir-it oft-en grieves; When our weep-ing's o-ver,

and the time of reap-ing, We shall come re-joic-ing, bring-ing in the sheaves.
and the la-bor end-ed, We shall come re-joic-ing, bring-ing in the sheaves.
He will bid us wel-come, We shall come re-joic-ing, bring-ing in the sheaves.

CHORUS

Bring-ing in the sheaves, bring-ing in the sheaves, We shall come re-joic-
Bring-ing in the sheaves, bring-ing in the sheaves, We shall come re-joic-

1.
ing, bring-ing in the sheaves;

2.
ing, bring-ing in the sheaves.

53   # SOMEBODY

G. V. T.

GORDON V. THOMPSON

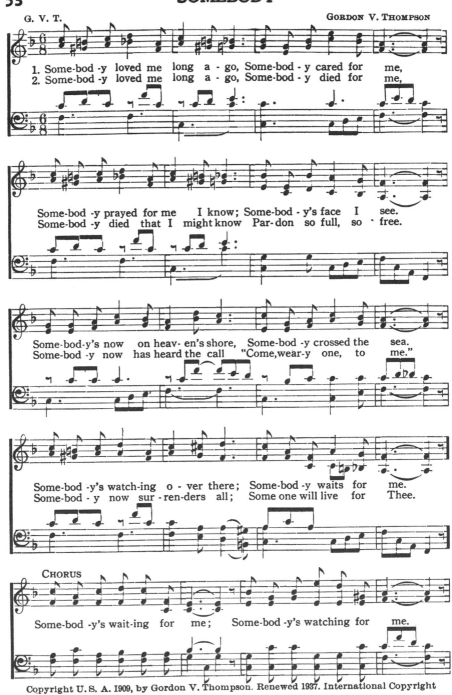

1. Some-bod-y loved me long a-go, Some-bod-y cared for me,
2. Some-bod-y loved me long a-go, Some-bod-y died for me,

Some-bod-y prayed for me I know; Some-bod-y's face I see.
Some-bod-y died that I might know Par-don so full, so free.

Some-bod-y's now on heav-en's shore, Some-bod-y crossed the sea.
Some-bod-y now has heard the call "Come, wear-y one, to me."

Some-bod-y's watch-ing o-ver there; Some-bod-y waits for me.
Some-bod-y now sur-ren-ders all; Some one will live for Thee.

CHORUS

Some-bod-y's wait-ing for me; Some-bod-y's watching for me.

SOMEBODY

Some-bod-y's wait-ing, some-bod-y's watching, Watching and waiting for me.

54 I AM COMING, LORD

L.H.

L. HARTSOUGH

1. I hear Thy wel-come voice, That calls me, Lord, to Thee, For
2. Tho' com-ing weak and vile, Thou dost my strength as-sure; Thou
3. 'Tis Je - sus calls me on To per-fect faith and love, To

cleans-ing in Thy prec-ious blood That flowed on Cal-va - ry.
dost my vile-ness ful - ly cleanse, Till spot-less all and pure.
per - fect hope, and peace, and trust, For earth and heav'n a - bove.

CHORUS

I am com-ing, Lord, Com - ing now to Thee!

Wash me, cleanse me, in the blood That flowed on Cal-va - ry!

55 WHITER THAN SNOW

JAMES NICHOLSON

WILLIAM G. FISCHER

1. Lord Je - sus, I long to be per - fect - ly whole; I want Thee for -
2. Lord Je - sus, look down from Thy throne in the skies, And help me to
3. Lord Je - sus, for this I most hum - bly en - treat; I wait, bless - ed
4. Lord Je - sus, Thou seest I pa - tient - ly wait; Come now, and with -

ev - er, to live in my soul; Break down ev - 'ry i - dol, cast
make a com - plete sac - ri - fice; I give up my - self, and what-
Lord, at Thy cru - ci - fied feet, By faith, for my cleansing I
in me a new heart cre - ate; To those who have sought Thee, Thou

out ev - 'ry foe; Now wash me, and I shall be whit - er than snow.
ev - er I know: Now wash me, and I shall be whit - er than snow.
see Thy blood flow: Now wash me, and I shall be whit - er than snow.
nev - er said'st No: Now wash me, and I shall be whit - er than snow.

CHORUS

Whit - er than snow, yes, whit - er than snow;

Now wash me, and I shall be whit - er than snow.

56 TELL ME THE OLD, OLD STORY

KATE HANKEY

W. H. DOANE

1. Tell me the Old, Old Sto - ry, Of un-seen things a - bove, Of Je-sus
2. Tell me the sto - ry slow - ly, That I may take it in— That won-der-
3. Tell me the sto - ry soft - ly, With earnest tones and grave; Re-mem-ber
4. Tell me the same old sto - ry, When you have cause to fear That this world's

and His glo - ry, Of Je - sus and His love; Tell me the sto - ry
ful re - demp-tion, God's rem - e - dy for sin; Tell me the sto - ry
I'm the sin - ner Whom Je - sus came to save; Tell me the sto - ry
emp-ty glo - ry Is cost - ing me too dear; Yes, and when that world's

sim - ply, As to a lit - tle child, For I am weak and wea - ry,
oft - en, For I for-get so soon, The "ear-ly dew" of morn-ing
al - ways If you would really be, In an - y time of troub - le,
glo - ry is dawning on my soul, Tell me the Old, Old Sto - ry:

CHORUS

And help - less and de - filed.
Has passed a - way at noon. Tell me the Old, Old Sto - ry, Tell me the
A com - fort - er to me.
"Christ Je - sus makes thee whole."

Old, Old Sto - ry, Tell me the Old, Old Sto - ry Of Je-sus and His love,

57 RESCUE THE PERISHING

FANNY J. CROSBY

WILLIAM H. DOANE

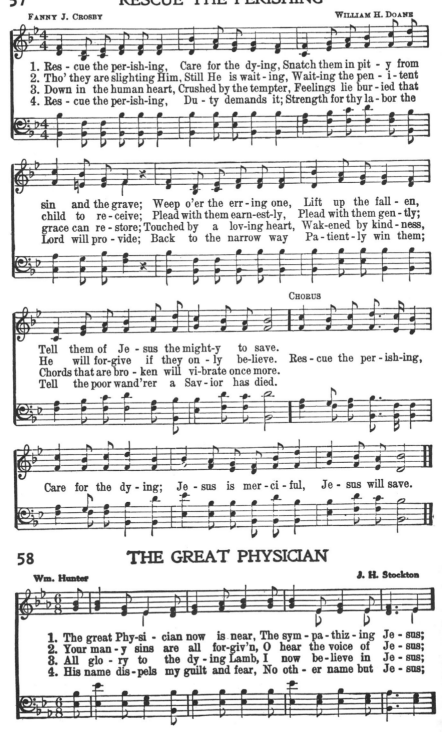

1. Res - cue the per-ish-ing, Care for the dy-ing, Snatch them in pit - y from
2. Tho' they are slighting Him, Still He is wait-ing, Wait-ing the pen - i - tent
3. Down in the human heart, Crushed by the tempter, Feelings lie bur - ied that
4. Res - cue the per-ish-ing, Du - ty demands it; Strength for thy la - bor the

sin and the grave; Weep o'er the err - ing one, Lift up the fall - en,
child to re - ceive; Plead with them earn-est-ly, Plead with them gen - tly;
grace can re - store; Touched by a lov-ing heart, Wak-ened by kind - ness,
Lord will pro - vide; Back to the narrow way Pa - tient-ly win them;

CHORUS

Tell them of Je - sus the might-y to save.
He will for-give if they on - ly be-lieve. Res - cue the per - ish-ing,
Chords that are bro - ken will vi-brate once more.
Tell the poor wand'rer a Sav-ior has died.

Care for the dy - ing; Je - sus is mer - ci - ful, Je - sus will save.

58 THE GREAT PHYSICIAN

Wm. Hunter

J. H. Stockton

1. The great Phy-si - cian now is near, The sym - pa - thiz-ing Je - sus;
2. Your man - y sins are all for-giv'n, O hear the voice of Je - sus;
3. All glo - ry to the dy - ing Lamb, I now be-lieve in Je - sus;
4. His name dis-pels my guilt and fear, No oth - er name but Je - sus;

THE GREAT PHYSICIAN

He speaks the droop-ing heart to cheer, O hear the voice of Je - sus.
Go on your way in peace to heav'n, And wear a crown with Je - sus.
I love the bless-ed Sav-ior's name, I love the name of Je - sus.
Oh! how my soul de-lights to hear The charming name of Je - sus.

D. S.—Sweet-est car - ol ev - er sung, Je - sus, bless-ed Je - sus.

REFRAIN

Sweet-est note in ser - aph song, Sweet-est name on mor - tal tongue,

JESUS LOVES ME

59

(The favorite Hymn of China)

WILLIAM B. BRADBURY

1. Je - sus loves me! this I know, For the Bi - ble tells me so;
2. Je - sus loves me! He who died, Heav-en's gates to o - pen wide;
3. Je - sus loves me! loves me still, Tho' I'm ver - y weak and ill;
4. Je - sus loves me! He will stay Close be - side me all the way;

Lit - tle ones to Him belong, They are weak, but He is strong.
He will wash a - way my sin, Let His lit - tle child come in. Yes, Je-sus
From His shining throne on high, Comes to watch me where I lie.
If I love Him when I die, He will take me home on high.

CHORUS

loves me, Yes, Jesus loves me, Yes, Jesus loves me, The Bi-ble tells me so.

LORD I'M COMING HOME

W. J. K.   Wm. J. Kirkpatrick.

1. I've wan-dered far a - way from God, Now I'm com-ing home;
2. I've wast - ed man - y pre - cious years, Now I'm com-ing home;
3. I've tired of sin and stray-ing, Lord, Now I'm com-ing home;
4. My soul is sick, my heart is sore, Now I'm com-ing home;
5. My on - ly hope, my on - ly plea, Now I'm com-ing home;
6. I need His cleans-ing blood, I know, Now I'm com-ing home;

The paths of sin too long I've trod, Lord, I'm com-ing home.
I now re-pent with bit - ter tears, Lord, I'm com-ing home.
I'll trust Thy love, be - lieve Thy word, Lord, I'm com-ing home.
My strength re-new, my hope re - store, Lord, I'm com-ing home.
That Je - sus died, and died for me, Lord, I'm com-ing home.
O wash me whit - er than the snow, Lord, I'm com-ing home.

CHORUS.

Com - ing home, com - ing home, Nev - er - more to roam,

O - pen wide Thine arms of love, Lord, I'm com-ing home.   A - MEN.

61   I LOVE TO TELL THE STORY

KATHERINE HANKEY   WILLIAM G. FISCHER

1. I love to tell the sto-ry Of un-seen things a-bove, Of Je-sus
2. I love to tell the sto-ry; More won-der-ful it seems Than all the
3. I love to tell the sto-ry; 'Tis pleas-ant to re-peat What seems each
4. I love to tell the sto-ry; For those who know it best Seem hun-ger-

and His glo-ry, Of Je-sus and His love, I love to tell the sto-ry,
gold-en fan-cies Of all our golden dreams. I love to tell the sto-ry,
time I tell it, More won-der-ful-ly sweet. I love to tell the sto-ry;
ing and thirsting To hear it like the rest. And when, in scenes of glo-ry,

Because I know 'tis true, It sat-is-fies my longings, As nothing else can do.
It did so much for me; And that is just the rea-son I tell it now to thee
For some have never heard The message of salvation From God's own holy word.
I sing the new, new song, 'Twill be the old, old story, That I have loved so long.

CHORUS

I love to tell the sto-ry! 'Twill be my theme in glo-ry

To tell the old, old sto-ry Of Je-sus and His love.

62 MORE LOVE TO THEE

ELIZABETH PRENTISS

W. H. DOANE

1. More love to Thee, O Christ, More love to Thee! Hear Thou the
2. Once earth-ly joy I craved, Sought peace and rest; Now Thee a-
3. Then shall my lat-est breath Whis-per Thy praise; This be the

pray'r I make On bend-ed knee; This is my earn-est plea:
lone I seek, Give what is best; This all my pray'r shall be:
part-ing cry My heart shall raise; This still its pray'r shall be:

More love, O Christ, to Thee, More love to Thee, More love to Thee!

63 O ZION, HASTE

MARY A. THOMSON

JAMES WALCH

1. O Zi-on, haste, thy mis-sion high ful-fill-ing, To tell to all the
2. Be-hold how ma-ny thousand still are ly-ing, Bound in the dark-some
3. Proclaim to ev-'ry peo-ple, tongue and na-tion That God in whom they
4. Give of thy sons to bear the message glo-rious; Give of thy wealth to

world that God is Light; That He who made all na-tions is not will-ing
pris-on-house of sin, With none to tell them of the Sav-ior's dy-ing,
live and move is love: Tell how He stooped to save His lost cre-a-tion,
speed them on their way; Pour out thy soul for them in pray'r vic-to-rious;

O ZION, HASTE

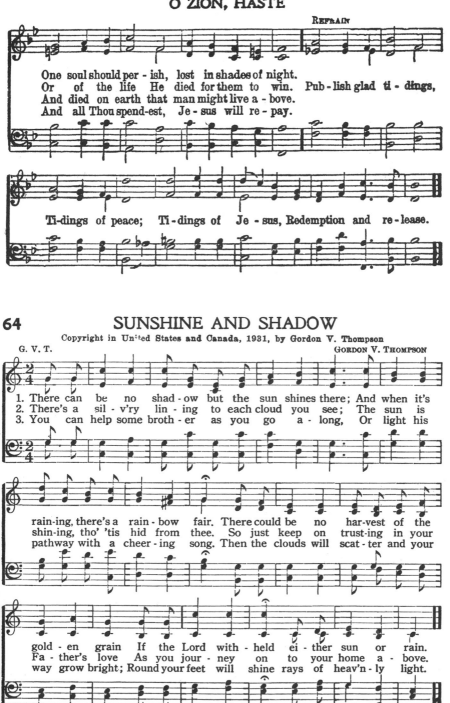

One soul should per-ish, lost in shades of night.
Or of the life He died for them to win. Pub-lish glad ti-dings,
And died on earth that man might live a-bove.
And all Thou spend-est, Je-sus will re-pay.

Ti-dings of peace; Ti-dings of Je-sus, Redemption and re-lease.

SUNSHINE AND SHADOW

64

Copyright in United States and Canada, 1931, by Gordon V. Thompson

G. V. T.

GORDON V. THOMPSON

1. There can be no shad-ow but the sun shines there; And when it's
2. There's a sil-v'ry lin-ing to each cloud you see; The sun is
3. You can help some broth-er as you go a-long, Or light his

rain-ing, there's a rain-bow fair. There could be no har-vest of the
shin-ing, tho' 'tis hid from thee. So just keep on trust-ing in your
pathway with a cheer-ing song. Then the clouds will scat-ter and your

gold-en grain If the Lord with-held ei-ther sun or rain.
Fa-ther's love As you jour-ney on to your home a-bove.
way grow bright; Round your feet will shine rays of heav'n-ly light.

THE NINETY AND NINE

E. C. CLEPHANE

IRA D. SANKEY

1. There were ninety and nine that safe - ly lay In the shel - ter of the fold,
2. "Lord, Thou hast here Thy ninety and nine; Are they not e - nough for Thee?"
3. But none of the ransomed ev - er knew How deep were the wa-ters cross'd;
4. "Lord, whence are those blood-drops all the way That mark out the mountain's track?"
5. But all thro' the mountains, thunder-riv'n, And up from the rock-y steep,

But one was out on the hills a - way, Far off from the gates of
But the Shepherd made an - swer: "This of mine Has wandered a - way from
Nor how dark was the night that the Lord pass'd thro' Ere He found His sheep that was
"They were shed for one who had gone a-stray Ere the Shepherd could bring him
There a - rose a great cry to the gate of heav'n, "Re - joice! I have found my

gold— A - way on the moun - tains wild and bare, A - way from the
me, And, al - though the road be rough and steep, I go to the
lost": Out in the des - ert He heard its cry— Sick and
back": "Lord, whence are Thy hands so rent and torn?" "They are pierced to-
sheep!" And the an - gels ech-oed a - round the throne, "Re - joice! for the

rit.

ten - der Shepherd's care, A - way from the ten - der Shep-herd's care.
des - ert to find my sheep, I go to the des-ert to find my sheep."
help-less, and read-y to die, Sick and helpless, and read-y to die.
night by man - y a thorn, They are pierced to- night by man-y a thorn."
Lord brings back His own! Re - joice! for the Lord brings back His own!"

SUNSHINE IN THE SOUL

E. E. HEWITT

JNO. R. SWENEY

67 I'LL GO WHERE YOU WANT ME TO GO

MARY BROWN   CARRIE E. ROUNSEFELL

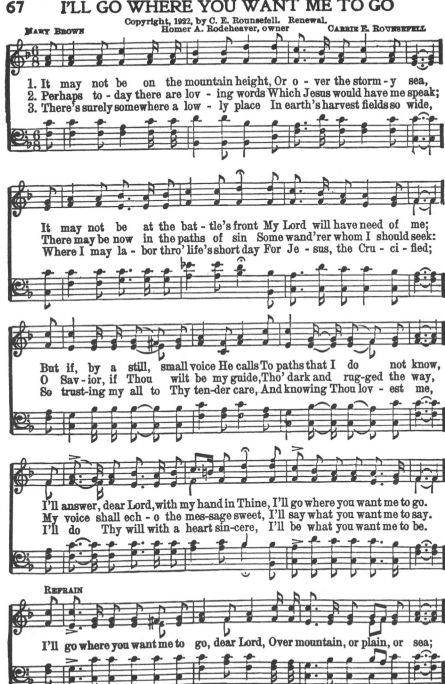

1. It may not be on the mountain height, Or o-ver the storm-y sea,
2. Perhaps to-day there are lov-ing words Which Jesus would have me speak;
3. There's surely somewhere a low-ly place In earth's harvest fields so wide,

It may not be at the bat-tle's front My Lord will have need of me;
There may be now in the paths of sin Some wand'rer whom I should seek:
Where I may la-bor thro' life's short day For Je-sus, the Cru-ci-fied;

But if, by a still, small voice He calls To paths that I do not know,
O Sav-ior, if Thou wilt be my guide, Tho' dark and rug-ged the way,
So trust-ing my all to Thy ten-der care, And knowing Thou lov-est me,

I'll answer, dear Lord, with my hand in Thine, I'll go where you want me to go.
My voice shall ech-o the mes-sage sweet, I'll say what you want me to say.
I'll do Thy will with a heart sin-cere, I'll be what you want me to be.

REFRAIN

I'll go where you want me to go, dear Lord, Over mountain, or plain, or sea;

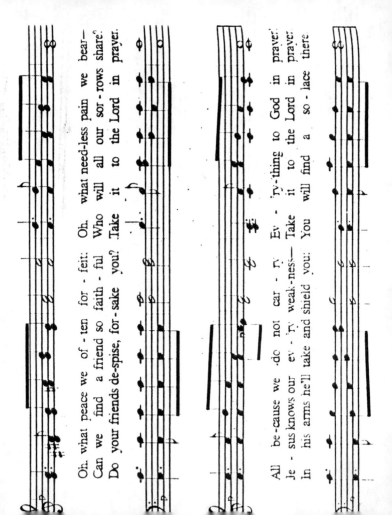

Oh, what peace we of-ten for-feit: Oh, what need-less pain we bear—
Can we find a friend so faith-ful Who will all our sor-rows share?
Do your friends de-spise, for-sake you? Take it to the Lord in prayer.

All be-cause we do not car-ry Ev-'ry-thing to God in prayer!
Je - sus knows our ev-'ry weak-ness— Take it to the Lord in prayer.
In his arms he'll take and shield you: You will find a so-lace there.

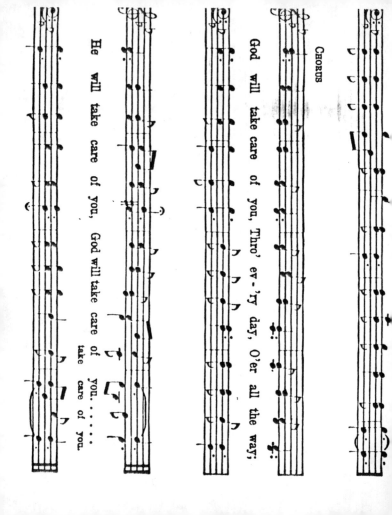

16

GOD WILL TAKE CARE OF YOU

(Dedicated to my wife, Mrs. John A. Davis)

C. D. MARTIN

W. S. MARTIN

1. Be not dis - mayed whate'er be - tide, God will take care of you;
2. Thro' days of toil when heart doth fail, God will take care of you;
3. All you may need He will pro - vide, God will take care of you;
4. No mat - ter what may be the test, God will take care of you;

Be - neath His wings of love a - bide, God will take care of you.
When dangers fierce your path as - sail, God will take care of you.

What a Friend We Have in Jesus

1 What a friend we have in Je - sus, All our sins and griefs to bear!
2 Have we tri - als and temp-ta - tions? Is there trou-ble an - y - where?
3 Are we weak and heav - y - lad - en, Cum - bered with a load of care?

What a priv - i - lege to car - ry Ev - 'ry-thing to God in prayer!
We should nev - er be dis-cour-aged— Take it to the Lord in prayer.
Pre-cious Sav - ior, still our ref - uge— Take it to the Lord in prayer.

I'LL GO WHERE YOU WANT ME TO GO

I'll say what you want me to say, dear Lord, I'll be what you want me to be.

68   NEAR THE CROSS

FANNY J. CROSBY   W. H. DOANE

1. Je - sus, keep me near the cross, There a pre - cious foun - tain
2. Near the cross, a trem-bling soul, Love and mer - cy found me;
3. Near the cross! O Lamb of God, Bring its scenes be - fore me;
4. Near the cross I'll watch and wait, Hop - ing, trust-ing ev - er,

Free to all— a heal - ing stream, Flows from Cal-v'ry's moun - tain.
There the Bright and Morn - ing Star Sheds its beams a - round me.
Help me walk from day to day, With its shad-ows o'er me.
Till I reach the gold - en strand, Just be - yond the riv - er.

CHORUS

In the cross, in the cross, Be my glo - ry ev - er;

Till my rap-tured soul shall find Rest be - yond the riv - er.

THE CAPTAIN IS CALLING

Elsie Duncan Yale

J. Lincoln Hall

1. In the ranks so true there's a place for you, The Cap-tain is call-ing;
2. To a con-flict long 'gainst a foe so strong, The Cap-tain is call-ing;
3. To a rich re-ward by His wondrous word, The Cap-tain is call-ing;

He calls, He calls;

Then en-list to-day, serve Him while you may, The Captain calls for you.
As a com-rade brave come the lost to save, The Captain calls for you.
Win a crown of life when shall end earth's strife, The Captain calls for you.

for you.

CHORUS.
Sop. and Altos.

For comrades loy-al-heart-ed ev-er, The Cap-tain is call-ing, O

Male Voices.

come with glad and true en-deav-or, The Captain calls for you. Then en-

list beneath His standard roy-al, Then be read-y both to dare and do,

THE CAPTAIN IS CALLING

All Parts.

The Cap-tain is call-ing, He calls for you.
He calls, the Cap-tain calls for you.

70   WHAT DID HE DO

Dr. J. M. Gray   W. Owen

1. O lis-ten to our wondrous sto - ry, Count-ed once a-mong the lost;
2. No an-gel could His place have tak-en, High-est of the high tho' he;
3. Will you sur-ren-der to this Sav - ior? To His scep-ter hum-bly bow?

Yet One came down from heaven's glo - ry, Sav-ing us at aw - ful cost!
The loved One on the cross for-sak - en Was One of the God-head three!
You, too, shall come to know His fa - vor, He will save you, save you now.

CHORUS.

Who saved us from e-ter - nal loss?   What did He do?
Who but God's Son up-on the cross?   He

Where is He now?   In heav - en in - ter - ced - ing!
died for you!   Be - lieve it thou, In heav - en in - ter - ced - ing!

TO THE WORK

Fanny J. Crosby

W. H. Deane

1. To the work! to the work! we are serv-ants of God, Let us fol-low the
2. To the work! to the work! let the hun-gry be fed, To the foun-tain of
3. To the work! to the work! there is la-bor for all; For the king-dom of
4. To the work! to the work in the strength of the Lord, And a robe and a

path that our Mas-ter has trod; With the balm of His coun-sel our
life let the wea-ry be led; In the cross and its ban-ner our
dark-ness and er-ror shall fall; And the name of Je-ho-vah ex-
crown shall our la-bor re-ward, When the home of the faith-ful our

strength to re-new, Let us do with our might what our hands find to do.
glo-ry shall be, While we her-ald the ti-dings, "Sal-va-tion is free!"
alt-ed shall be, In the loud-swell-ing cho-rus, "Sal-va-tion is free!"
dwell-ing shall be, And we shout with the ransomed, "Sal-va-tion is free!"

CHORUS.

Toil-ing on, Toil-ing on, toil-ing on, toil-ing on, Toil-ing

on, Toil-ing on, toil-ing on, toil-ing on; Let us hope and trust,

let us watch, and pray, And la-bor till the Mas-ter comes.

72 SOME DAY HE'LL MAKE IT PLAIN

Lida Shivers Leech

Adam Geibel.

Solo, or all in unison.

1. I do not know why oft 'round me My hopes all shattered seem to be;
2. I can-not tell the depth of love, Which moves the Father's heart a-bove;
3. Tho' tri-als come thro' passing days, My life will still be filled with praise;

God's perfect plan I can-not see, ...But some day I'll un-der-stand.
My faith to test, my love to prove, ...But some day I'll un-der-stand.
For God will lead thro' darkened ways , ..But some day I'll un-der-stand.

CHORUS.

Some day He'll make it plain to me, Some day when I His face shall see;

Some day from tears I shall be free, For some day I shall un-der-stand.

SOFTLY AND TENDERLY

W. L. T.

WILL L. THOMPSON

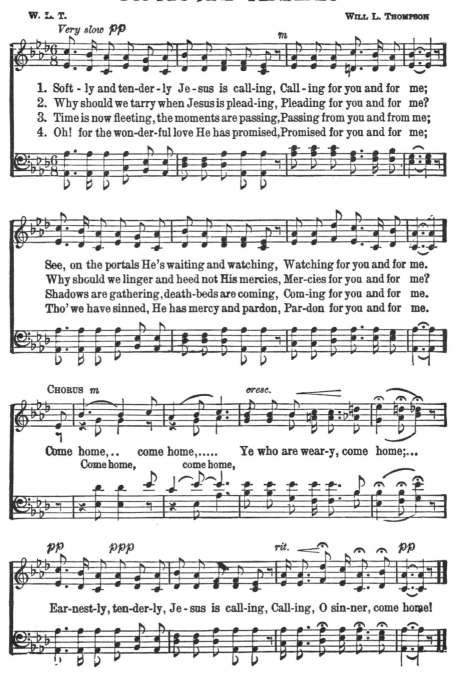

Very slow pp

m

1. Soft - ly and ten-der - ly Je - sus is call-ing, Call - ing for you and for me;
2. Why should we tarry when Jesus is plead-ing, Pleading for you and for me?
3. Time is now fleeting, the moments are passing, Passing from you and from me;
4. Oh! for the won-der-ful love He has promised, Promised for you and for me;

See, on the portals He's waiting and watching, Watching for you and for me.
Why should we linger and heed not His mercies, Mer-cies for you and for me?
Shadows are gathering, death-beds are coming, Com-ing for you and for me.
Tho' we have sinned, He has mercy and pardon, Par-don for you and for me.

CHORUS m

cresc.

Come home,.. come home,...... Ye who are wear-y, come home;...
Come home, come home,

pp   ppp   rit.   pp

Ear-nest-ly, ten-der-ly, Je - sus is call-ing, Call-ing, O sin-ner, come home!

74 O JESUS, THOU ART STANDING

WILLIAM W. HOW

JUSTIN H. KNECHT

1. O Je - sus, Thou art stand - ing Out - side the fast-closed door,
2. O Je - sus, Thou art knock - ing; And lo, that hand is scarred,
3. O Je - sus, Thou art plead - ing In ac - cents meek and low,

In low - ly pa-tience wait - ing To pass the thresh - old o'er:
And thorns Thy brow en - cir - cle, And tears Thy face have marred:
"I died for you, my chil - dren, And will you treat Me so?"

Shame on us, Chris-tian broth - ers, His name and sign who bear,
O love that pass - eth knowl - edge, So pa - tient - ly to wait!
O Lord, with shame and sor - row We o - pen now the door;

O shame, thrice shame up - on us, To keep Him stand - ing there!
O sin that hath no e - qual, So fast to bar the gate!
Dear Sav - ior, en - ter, en - ter, And leave us nev - er - more.

75 SAFELY THROUGH ANOTHER WEEK

JOHN NEWTON

LOWELL MASON

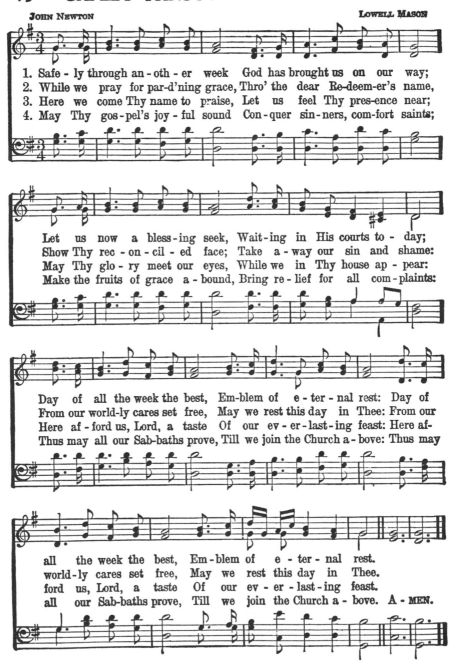

1. Safe - ly through an - oth - er week God has brought us on our way;
2. While we pray for par-d'ning grace, Thro' the dear Re-deem-er's name,
3. Here we come Thy name to praise, Let us feel Thy pres-ence near;
4. May Thy gos-pel's joy - ful sound Con - quer sin - ners, com-fort saints;

Let us now a bless-ing seek, Wait-ing in His courts to - day;
Show Thy rec - on - cil - ed face; Take a - way our sin and shame:
May Thy glo - ry meet our eyes, While we in Thy house ap - pear:
Make the fruits of grace a - bound, Bring re - lief for all com - plaints:

Day of all the week the best, Em-blem of e - ter - nal rest: Day of
From our world-ly cares set free, May we rest this day in Thee: From our
Here af - ford us, Lord, a taste Of our ev - er - last-ing feast: Here af-
Thus may all our Sab-baths prove, Till we join the Church a - bove: Thus may

all the week the best, Em-blem of e - ter - nal rest.
world-ly cares set free, May we rest this day in Thee.
ford us, Lord, a taste Of our ev - er - last-ing feast.
all our Sab-baths prove, Till we join the Church a - bove. A - MEN.

76 LEANING ON THE EVERLASTING ARMS

REV. E. A. HOFFMAN

A. J. SHOWALTER

1. What a fel - low - ship, what a joy Di - vine, Lean - ing
2. O how sweet to walk in this pil - grim way, Lean - ing
3. What have I to dread, what have I to fear, Lean - ing

on the Ev - er - last - ing Arms! What a bless - ed - ness, what a peace is mine,
on the Ev - er - last - ing Arms! O how bright the path grows from day to day,
on the Ev - er - last - ing Arms! I have peace complete with my Lord so near,

REFRAIN

Lean - ing on the Ev - er - last - ing Arms! Lean - - ing,
Lean - ing on Je - sus,

lean - - ing, Safe and secure from all a - larms; Lean - - ing,
Lean - ing on Je - sus, Lean - ing on Je - sus,

lean - - ing, Lean - ing on the Ev - er - last - ing Arms.
Lean - ing on Je - sus,

77 WHO IS ON THE LORD'S SIDE

Frances R. Havergal

Arranged by John Goss

1. Who is on the Lord's side? Who will serve the King? Who will be His help-ers
2. Not for weight of glo - ry, Not for crown and palm, En-ter we the ar - my,
3. Je - sus, Thou hast bought us, Not with gold or gem, But with Thine own life-blood,
4. Fierce may be the con - flict, Strong may be the foe, But the King's own ar-my

Oth - er lives to bring? Who will leave the world's side? Who will face the foe?
Raise the war-rior psalm; But for love that claim-eth Lives for whom He died:
For Thy di - a - dem: With Thy blessing fill - ing Each who comes to Thee,
None can o - ver-throw: Round His standard rang-ing, Vic-t'ry is se-cure;

Who is on the Lord's side? Who for Him will go? By Thy call of mer - cy,
He whom Je - sus nam-eth Must be on His side. By Thy love constraining,
Thou hast made us will-ing, Thou hast made us free. By Thy grand re-demp-tion,
For His truth un-chang-ing Makes the tri-umph sure. Joy-ful - ly en - list - ing,

By Thy grace di-vine, We are on the Lord's side, Sav - ior, we are Thine. A-MEN.

78 COME TO THE SAVIOR

G. F. R.

George F. Root

1. Come to the Sav-ior, make no de-lay; Here in His Word He's shown us the way;
2. "Suf - fer the children!" Oh, hear His voice, Let ev'ry heart leap forth and re-joice.
3. Think once again, He's with us to-day; Heed now His blest commands, and o-bey;

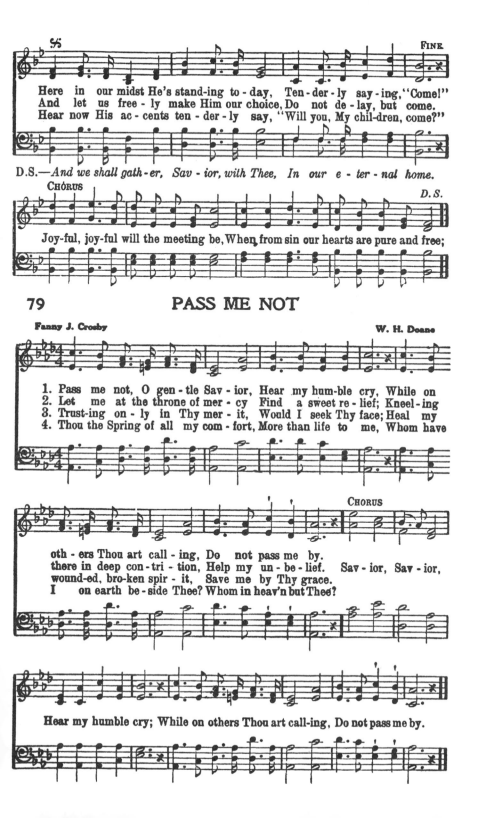

80 CARRY THY BURDEN TO JESUS

Ethel Verne King

Robert Hood Bowers

Allegretto moderato.

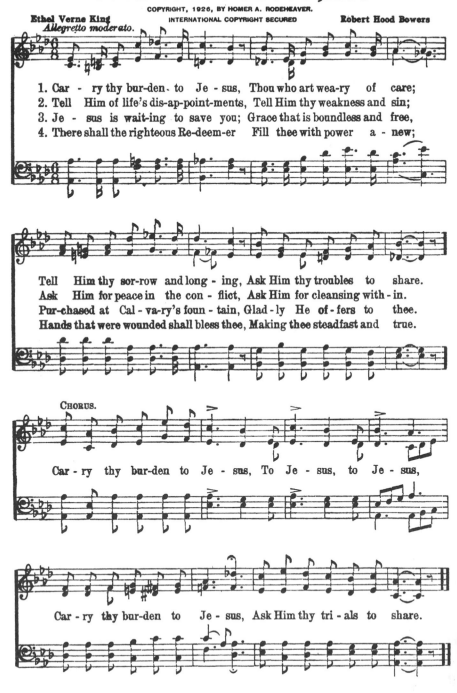

1. Car - ry thy bur-den. to Je - sus, Thou who art wea-ry of care;
2. Tell Him of life's dis-ap-point-ments, Tell Him thy weakness and sin;
3. Je - sus is wait-ing to save you; Grace that is boundless and free,
4. There shall the righteous Re-deem-er Fill thee with power a - new;

Tell Him thy sor-row and long - ing, Ask Him thy troubles to share.
Ask Him for peace in the con - flict, Ask Him for cleansing with-in.
Pur-chased at Cal - va-ry's foun - tain, Glad-ly He of-fers to thee.
Hands that were wounded shall bless thee, Making thee steadfast and true.

CHORUS.

Car - ry thy bur-den to Je - sus, To Je - sus, to Je - sus,

Car - ry thy bur-den to Je - sus, Ask Him thy tri - als to share.

THE NAME OF JESUS

W. C. Martin   E. S. Lorenz

1. The name of Je - sus is so sweet, I love its mu - sic
2. I love the name of Him whose heart Knows all my griefs and
3. That name I fond - ly love to hear, It nev - er fails my
4. No word of man can ev - er tell How sweet the name I

to re - peat; It makes my joys full and com - plete, The pre - cious
bears a part; Who bids all an - xious fears de - part— I love the
heart to cheer, Its mu - sic dries the fall - ing tear; Ex - alt the
love so well, Oh, let its prais - es ev - er swell, Oh, praise the

CHORUS

name of Je - sus. "Je - sus," oh, how sweet the name!
pre - cious name,

"Je - sus," ev - 'ry day the same; "Je - sus," let all

saints pro - claim its wor - thy praise for - ev - er.
Its wor - thy praise

CHARLOTTE ELLIOTT   WILLIAM B. BRADBURY

1. Just as I am, with-out one plea, But that Thy blood was shed for me,
2. Just as I am, and waiting not To rid my soul of one dark blot,
3. Just as I am, tho' tossed a-bout With many a con-flict, many a doubt,
4. Just as I am, poor, wretched, blind; Sight, rich-es, heal-ing of the mind,
5. Just as I am—Thou wilt re-ceive, Wilt welcome, pardon, cleanse, relieve;

And that Thou bidd'st me come to Thee, O Lamb of God, I come! I come!
To Thee whose blood can cleanse each spot, O Lamb of God, I come! I come!
Fight-ings and fears with-in, with-out, O Lamb of God, I come! I come!
Yea, all I need in Thee to find, O Lamb of God, I come! I come!
Be - cause Thy promise I be-lieve, O Lamb of God, I come! I come!

83   REVIVE US AGAIN

Wm. P. Mackay   John J. Husband

1. We praise Thee, O God! for the Son of Thy love, For Je - sus who
2. We praise Thee, O God! for Thy Spir - it of light, Who has shown us our
3. All glo - ry and praise to the Lamb that was slain, Who has borne all our
4. Re - vive us a - gain; fill each heart with Thy love; May each soul be re-

CHORUS

died, and is now gone a - bove.
Sav - ior, and scat-tered our night.   Hal-le - lu - jah! Thine the glo-ry, Hal-le-
sins, and has cleansed ev-'ry stain.
kin - dled with fire from a - bove.

REVIVE US AGAIN

lu-jah! a-men; Hal-le-lu-jah! Thine the glo-ry, re-vive us a-gain.

84

LEAD ME TO CALVARY

COPYRIGHT, 1921, BY HALL-MACK CO.
INTERNATIONAL COPYRIGHT SECURED

Jennie Evelyn Hussey

Wm. J. Kirkpatrick

1. King of my life, I crown Thee now, Thine shall the glo-ry be;
2. Show me the tomb where Thou wast laid, Ten-der-ly mourned and wept;
3. Let me like Ma-ry, thru the gloom, Come with a gift to Thee;
4. May I be will-ing, Lord, to bear Dai-ly my cross for Thee;

Lest I for-get Thy thorn-crowned brow, Lead me to Cal-va-ry.
An-gels in robes of light ar-rayed Guard-ed Thee whilst Thou slept.
Show to me now the emp-ty tomb, Lead me to Cal-va-ry.
E-ven Thy cup of grief to share, Thou hast borne all for me.

CHORUS

Lest I for-get Geth-sem-a-ne; Lest I for-get Thine ag-o-ny;

Lest I for-get Thy love for me, Lead me to Cal-va-ry.

DOES JESUS CARE

Frank E. Graeff

J. Lincoln Hall

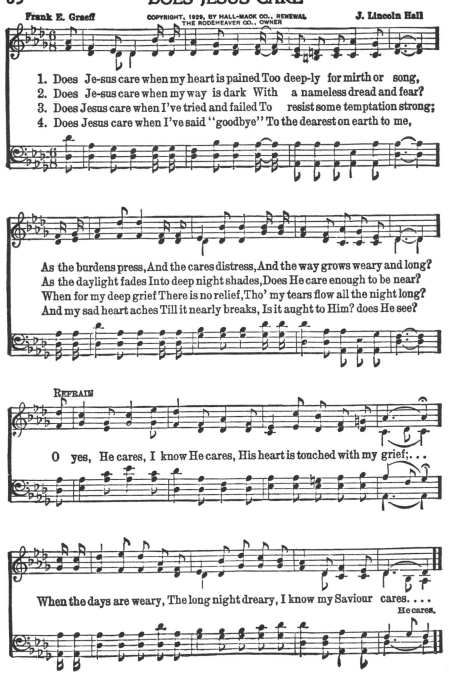

1. Does Je-sus care when my heart is pained Too deep-ly for mirth or song,
2. Does Je-sus care when my way is dark With a nameless dread and fear?
3. Does Jesus care when I've tried and failed To resist some temptation strong;
4. Does Jesus care when I've said "goodbye" To the dearest on earth to me,

As the burdens press, And the cares distress, And the way grows weary and long?
As the daylight fades Into deep night shades, Does He care enough to be near?
When for my deep grief There is no relief, Tho' my tears flow all the night long?
And my sad heart aches Till it nearly breaks, Is it aught to Him? does He see?

REFRAIN

O yes, He cares, I know He cares, His heart is touched with my grief;...

When the days are weary, The long night dreary, I know my Saviour cares. ....

He cares.

86   I WILL NOT FORGET THEE

C. H. G.   Chas. H. Gabriel

1. Sweet is the promise—"I will not for-get thee," Nothing can molest or
2. Trust-ing the promise—"I will not for-get thee," Onward will I go with
3. When at the gold-en por-tals I am standing, All my trib - u - la - tions,

turn my soul a - way: E'en tho' the night be dark with-in the val - ley,
songs of joy and love; Tho' earth de-spise me, tho' my friends forsake me,
all my sor-rows past. How sweet to hear the bless-ed proc - la - ma - tion,

CHORUS.

Just beyond is shining one e-ter-nal day. I . . . . will not forget thee or
I shall be remembered in my home above.
"Enter, faithful servant, welcome home at last!" I will not forget thee,   I will never

leave thee; In my hands I'll hold thee, in my arms I'll fold thee; I. . . . . . . will
leave thee;   I will not for-get

not for-get thee or leave thee, I am thy Redeem - er, I will care for thee.
thee, for-get

JESUS SAVES

Priscilla J. Owens

Wm. J. Kirkpatrick

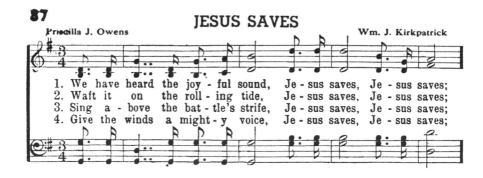

1. We have heard the joy - ful sound, Je - sus saves, Je - sus saves;
2. Waft it on the roll - ing tide, Je - sus saves, Je - sus saves;
3. Sing a - bove the bat - tle's strife, Je - sus saves, Je - sus saves;
4. Give the winds a might - y voice, Je - sus saves, Je - sus saves;

Spread the ti - dings all a - round, Je - sus saves, Je - sus saves;
Tell to sin - ners far and wide, Je - sus saves, Je - sus saves;
By His death and end - less life, Je - sus saves, Je - sus saves;
Let the na - tions now re - joice,— Je - sus saves, Je - sus saves;

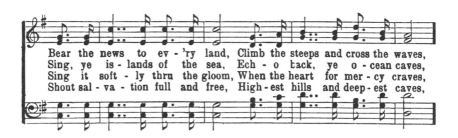

Bear the news to ev - 'ry land, Climb the steeps and cross the waves,
Sing, ye is - lands of the sea, Ech - o back, ye o - cean caves,
Sing it soft - ly thru the gloom, When the heart for mer - cy craves,
Shout sal - va - tion full and free, High - est hills and deep - est caves,

On - ward!—'tis our Lord's com - mand, Je - sus saves, Je - sus saves.
Earth shall keep her ju - bi - lee, Je - sus saves, Je - sus saves.
Sing in tri - umph o'er the tomb,— Je - sus saves, Je - sus saves.
This our song of vic - to - ry,— Je - sus saves, Je - sus saves.

"WHOSOEVER WILL"

P. P. B.

P. P. BLISS

1. "Who-so-ev-er hear - eth," shout, shout the sound! Spread the bless-ed ti-dings
2. Who-so-ev-er com - eth, need not de - lay, Now the door is o - pen,
3. "Who-so-ev-er will!" the prom-ise is se - cure; "Who-so-ev-er will," for-

all the world a-round; Tell the joy - ful news wher - ev - er man is found,
en - ter while you may; Je - sus is the true, the on - ly Liv - ing Way:
ev - er must en-dure; "Who-so - ev - er will!" 'tis life for - ev - er - more;

CHORUS

"Who-so-ev - er will may come." "Who-so-ev - er will, who - so-ev - er will!"

Send the proc - la - ma - tion o - ver vale and hill; 'Tis a lov - ing

Fa - ther calls the wan-d'rer home: "Who-so - ev - er will may come."

THE ROCK THAT IS HIGHER THAN I

E. JOHNSON   WILLIAM G. FISCHER

1. O some-times the shadows are deep, And rough seems the path to the goal,
2. O sometimes how long seems the day, And sometimes how wea-ry my feet;
3. O near to the Rock let me keep, If bless-ings or sor-rows pre-vail;

And sorrows, sometimes how they sweep Like tempests down o-ver the soul!
But toil-ing in life's dust-y way, The Rock's blessed shadow, how sweet!
Or climb-ing the mountain way steep, Or walk-ing the shad-ow-y vale.

REFRAIN

O then to' the Rock let me fly, let me fly, To the Rock that is high-er than I; is high-er than I; O then to the Rock let me fly, let me fly, To the Rock that is high-er than I!

HE'S THE ONE

J.B.M

J. B. MACKAY

1. Is there an-y-one can help us, one who un-der-stands our hearts When the
2. Is there an-y-one can help us when the load is hard to bear, And we
3. Is there an-y-one can help us who can give a sin-ner peace, When his
4. Is there an-y-one can help us, when the end is draw-ing near, Who will

thorns of life have pierced them till they bleed; One who sympathiz-es with us, who in
faint and fall be-neath it in a - larm; Who in ten-der-ness will lift us, and the
heart is burdened down with pain and woe; Who can speak the word of pardon that af-
go thro'death's dark waters by our side; Who will light the way before us, and dis-

won-drous love im-parts Just the ver-y, ver-y bless-ing that we need?
heav-y bur-den share, And sup-port us with an ev-er-last-ing arm?
fords a sweet re-lease, And whose blood can wash and make us white as snow?
pel all doubt and fear, And will bear our spir-its safe-ly o'er the tide?

CHORUS

Yes, there's One, on - ly One, The
Yes, there's One, on - ly One,

bless-ed, bless-ed Je-sus, He's the One; When af-flictions press the soul, when

waves of trouble roll, And you need a friend to help you, He's the One.

91 ALL THE WAY MY SAVIOR LEADS

Fanny J. Crosby   Robert Lowry

1. All the way my Sav-ior leads me; What have I to ask be-side?
2. All the way my Sav-ior leads me; Cheers each winding path I tread;
3. All the way my Sav-ior leads me; O the full-ness of His love!

Can I doubt His ten-der mer-cy Who thru life has been my guide?
Gives me grace for ev-'ry tri-al, Feeds me with the liv-ing bread;
Per-fect rest to me is prom-ised In my Fa-ther's house a-bove;

Heav'n-ly peace, di-vin-est com-fort, Here by faith in Him to dwell!
Tho' my wea-ry steps may fal-ter, And my soul a-thirst may be,
When my spir-it, clothed im-mor-tal, Wings its flight to realms of day,

For I know, what-e'er be-fall me, Je-sus do-eth all things well;
Gush-ing from the Rock be-fore me, Lo! a spring of joy I see;
This my song thru end-less a-ges—Je-sus led me all the way;

For I know, what-e'er be-fall me, Je-sus do-eth all things well.
Gush-ing from the Rock be-fore me, Lo! a spring of joy I see.
This my song thru end-less a-ges—Je-sus led me all the way.

92 IT IS WELL WITH MY SOUL

H. G. Spafford

P. P. Bliss

1. When peace, like a riv - er, at - tend-eth my way, When sor-rows like
2. Though Sa-tan should buf - fet, tho' tri - als should come, Let this blest as-
3. My sin— oh, the bliss of this glo - ri - ous tho't—My sin—not in
4. And, Lord, haste the day when the faith shall be sight, The clouds be rolled

sea - bil - lows roll; What-ev - er my lot, Thou hast taught me to say,
sur - ance con-trol, That Christ has re-gard - ed my help - less es - tate,
part, but the whole, Is nailed to the cross and I bear it no more,
back as a scroll, The trump shall re-sound and the Lord shall de-scend,

CHORUS

It is well, it is well with my soul.
And hath shed His own blood for my soul. It is well . . . . . with my
Praise the Lord, praise the Lord, O my soul!
"E - ven so"—it is well with my soul. It is well

soul, ... It is well, it is well with my soul.
with my soul,

MY REDEEMER

P. P. BLISS

JAMES McGRANAHAN

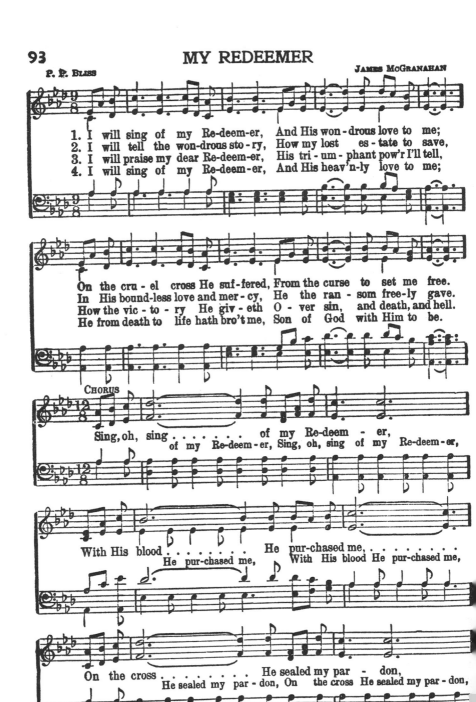

1. I will sing of my Re-deem-er, And His won-drous love to me;
2. I will tell the won-drous sto-ry, How my lost es-tate to save,
3. I will praise my dear Re-deem-er, His tri-um-phant pow'r I'll tell,
4. I will sing of my Re-deem-er, And His heav'n-ly love to me;

On the cru-el cross He suf-fered, From the curse to set me free.
In His bound-less love and mer-cy, He the ran-som free-ly gave.
How the vic-to-ry He giv-eth O-ver sin, and death, and hell.
He from death to life hath bro't me, Son of God with Him to be.

CHORUS

Sing, oh, sing . . . . of my Re-deem - er,
of my Re-deem-er, Sing, oh, sing of my Re-deem-er,

With His blood . . . . He pur-chased me, ...
He pur-chased me, With His blood He pur-chased me,

On the cross . . . . He sealed my par - don,
He sealed my par-don, On the cross He sealed my par-don,

94 TAKE THE NAME OF JESUS WITH YOU

Mrs. Lydia Baxter

W. H. Doane

1. Take the name of Je-sus with you, Child of sor-row and of woe;
2. Take the name of Je-sus ev - er, As a shield from ev-'ry snare;
3. O the precious name of Je - sus! How it thrills our souls with joy,
4. At the name of Je-sus bow-ing, Fall-ing pros-trate at His feet,

It will joy and com-fort give you, Take it, then, wher-e'er you go.
If temp-ta-tions round you gath-er, Breathe that ho - ly name in prayer.
When His lov-ing arms re-ceive us, And His songs our tongues em-ploy!
King of kings in Heav'n we'll crown Him, When our jour-ney is com-plete.

Chorus

Pre-cious name, O how sweet! Hope of earth and joy of Heav'n;
Precious name, O how sweet!

Pre-cious name, O how sweet!... Hope of earth and joy of Heav'n.
Precious name, O how sweet, how sweet!

S. O'MALEY CLUFF

IRA D. SANKEY

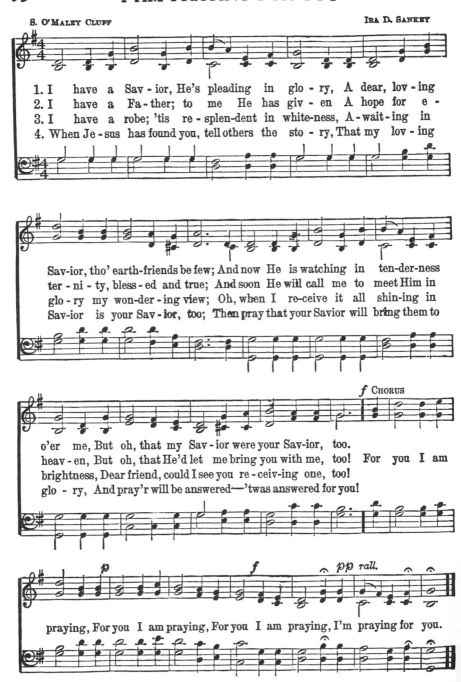

1. I have a Sav - ior, He's pleading in glo - ry, A dear, lov - ing
2. I have a Fa - ther; to me He has giv - en A hope for e -
3. I have a robe; 'tis re - splen-dent in white-ness, A - wait - ing in
4. When Je - sus has found you, tell others the sto - ry, That my lov - ing

Sav-ior, tho' earth-friends be few; And now He is watching in ten-der-ness
ter - ni - ty, bless - ed and true; And soon He will call me to meet Him in
glo - ry my won-der - ing view; Oh, when I re-ceive it all shin-ing in
Sav-ior is your Sav - ior, too; Then pray that your Savior will bring them to

f CHORUS

o'er me, But oh, that my Sav - ior were your Sav-ior, too.
heav - en, But oh, that He'd let me bring you with me, too! For you I am
brightness, Dear friend, could I see you re - ceiv-ing one, too!
glo - ry, And pray'r will be answered—'twas answered for you!

p   f   pp rall.

praying, For you I am praying, For you I am praying, I'm praying for you.

96

GOD WILL TAKE CARE OF YOU

(Dedicated to my wife, Mrs. John A. Davis)

C. D. MARTIN

W. S. MARTIN

1. Be not dis-mayed whate'er be-tide, God will take care of you;
2. Thro' days of toil when heart doth fail, God will take care of you;
3. All you may need He will pro-vide, God will take care of you;
4. No mat-ter what may be the test, God will take care of you;

Be-neath His wings of love a-bide, God will take care of you.
When dangers fierce your path as-sail, God will take care of you.
Noth-ing you ask will be de-nied, God will take care of you.
Lean, wea-ry one, up-on His breast, God will take care of you.

CHORUS

God will take care of you, Thro' ev-'ry day, O'er all the way;

He will take care of you, God will take care of you.....
take care of you.

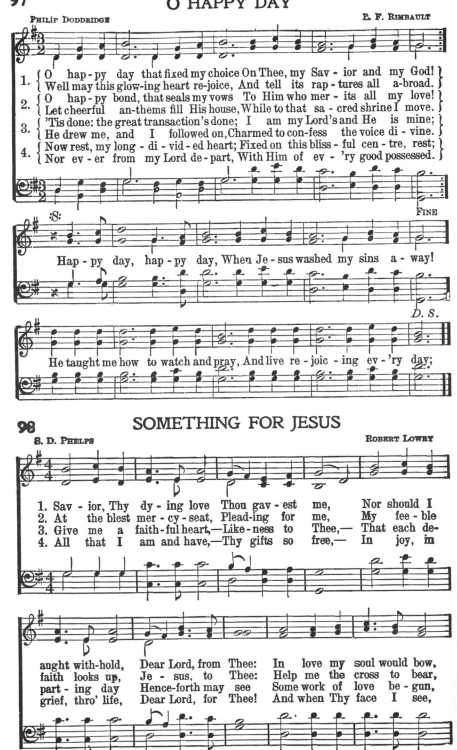

O HAPPY DAY

PHILIP DODDRIDGE

E. F. RIMBAULT

1. O hap-py day that fixed my choice On Thee, my Sav-ior and my God!
Well may this glow-ing heart re-joice, And tell its rap-tures all a-broad.

2. O hap-py bond, that seals my vows To Him who mer-its all my love!
Let cheerful an-thems fill His house, While to that sa-cred shrine I move.

3. 'Tis done: the great transaction's done; I am my Lord's and He is mine;
He drew me, and I followed on, Charmed to con-fess the voice di-vine.

4. Now rest, my long-di-vid-ed heart; Fixed on this bliss-ful cen-tre, rest;
Nor ev-er from my Lord de-part, With Him of ev-'ry good possessed.

FINE

Hap-py day, hap-py day, When Je-sus washed my sins a-way!

D. S.

He taught me how to watch and pray, And live re-joic-ing ev-'ry day;

SOMETHING FOR JESUS

S. D. PHELPS

ROBERT LOWRY

1. Sav-ior, Thy dy-ing love Thou gav-est me, Nor should I
2. At the blest mer-cy-seat, Plead-ing for me, My fee-ble
3. Give me a faith-ful heart,—Like-ness to Thee,— That each de-
4. All that I am and have,—Thy gifts so free,— In joy, in

aught with-hold, Dear Lord, from Thee: In love my soul would bow,
faith looks up, Je-sus, to Thee: Help me the cross to bear,
part-ing day, Hence-forth may see Some work of love be-gun,
grief, thro' life, Dear Lord, for Thee! And when Thy face I see,

SOMETHING FOR JESUS

My heart ful-fill its vow, Some of-f'ring bring Thee now, Something for Thee.
Thy wondrous love de-clare, Some song to raise, or prayer, Something for Thee.
Some deed of kind-ness done, Some wand'rer sought and won, Something for Thee.
My ransomed soul shall be, Thro' all e-ter-ni-ty, Something for Thee.

99 TRUSTING JESUS

E. Page

Ira D. Sankey

1. Sim - ply trust-ing ev - 'ry day, Trust-ing thru a storm-y way;
2. Bright-ly doth His Spir-it shine In - to this poor heart of mine;
3. Sing-ing if my way is clear; Pray-ing if the path be drear;
4. Trust-ing Him while life shall last, Trust-ing Him till earth be past;

E - ven when my faith is small, Trust-ing Je - sus, that is all.
While He leads I can-not fall; Trust-ing Je - sus, that is all.
If in dan - ger, for Him call; Trust-ing Je - sus, that is all.
Till with-in the jas - per wall: Trust-ing Je - sus, that is all.

CHORUS

Trust-ing as the mo-ments fly, Trust-ing as the days go by;

Trust-ing Him what-e'er be-fall, Trust-ing Je - sus, that is all.

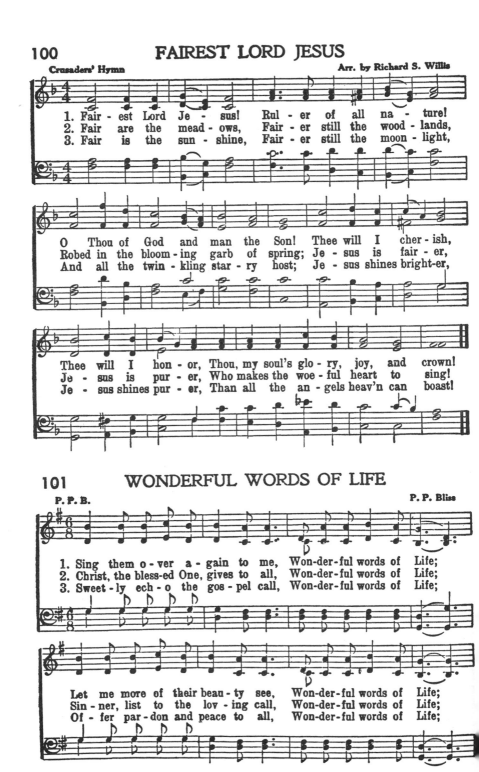

FAIREST LORD JESUS

100

Crusaders' Hymn

Arr. by Richard S. Willis

1. Fair - est Lord Je - sus! Rul - er of all na - ture!
2. Fair are the mead - ows, Fair - er still the wood - lands,
3. Fair is the sun - shine, Fair - er still the moon - light,

O Thou of God and man the Son! Thee will I cher - ish,
Robed in the bloom - ing garb of spring; Je - sus is fair - er,
And all the twin - kling star - ry host; Je - sus shines bright-er,

Thee will I hon - or, Thou, my soul's glo - ry, joy, and crown!
Je - sus is pur - er, Who makes the woe - ful heart to sing!
Je - sus shines pur - er, Than all the an - gels heav'n can boast!

WONDERFUL WORDS OF LIFE

101

P. P. B.

P. P. Bliss

1. Sing them o - ver a - gain to me, Won-der-ful words of Life;
2. Christ, the bless-ed One, gives to all, Won-der-ful words of Life;
3. Sweet-ly ech - o the gos - pel call, Won-der-ful words of Life;

Let me more of their beau - ty see, Won-der-ful words of Life;
Sin - ner, list to the lov - ing call, Won-der-ful words of Life;
Of - fer par - don and peace to all, Won-der-ful words of Life;

WONDERFUL WORDS OF LIFE

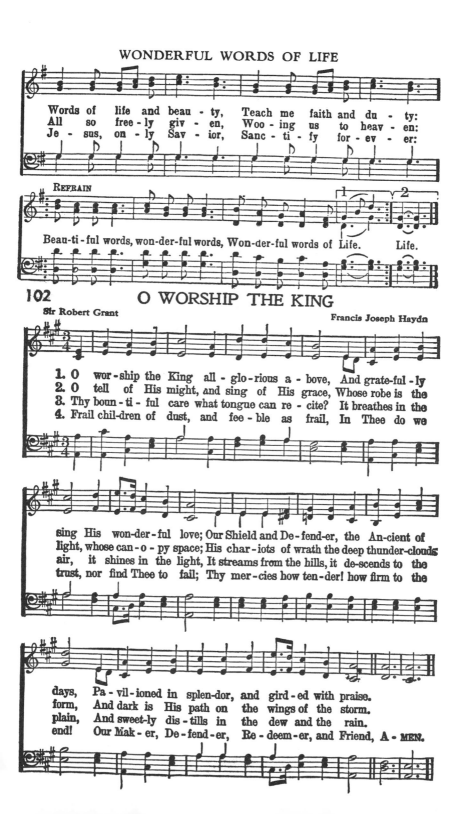

Words of life and beau - ty, Teach me faith and du - ty:
All so free - ly giv - en, Woo - ing us to heav - en:
Je - sus, on - ly Sav - ior, Sanc - ti - fy for - ev - er:

REFRAIN

Beau-ti - ful words, won-der-ful words, Won-der-ful words of Life. Life.

102   O WORSHIP THE KING

Sir Robert Grant   Francis Joseph Haydn

1. O wor - ship the King all - glo - rious a - bove, And grate-ful - ly
2. O tell of His might, and sing of His grace, Whose robe is the
3. Thy boun - ti - ful care what tongue can re - cite? It breathes in the
4. Frail chil-dren of dust, and fee - ble as frail, In Thee do we

sing His won-der - ful love; Our Shield and De-fend-er, the An-cient of
light, whose can - o - py space; His char - iots of wrath the deep thunder-clouds
air, it shines in the light, It streams from the hills, it de-scends to the
trust, nor find Thee to fail; Thy mer-cies how ten-der! how firm to the

days, Pa - vil - ioned in splen-dor, and gird - ed with praise.
form, And dark is His path on the wings of the storm.
plain, And sweet-ly dis - tills in the dew and the rain.
end! Our Mak - er, De - fend - er, Re - deem - er, and Friend, A - MEN.

THY YOKE

G.V.T.

GORDON V. THOMPSON

1. Lord, I would bear Thy yoke and learn of Thee,
2. Lord, I would tread the path Thy feet have trod,
3. So let me walk with Thee through-out the years;

So will my load of care and sor-row flee;
Fol - low Thee home to heav-en and to God;
Live in Thy love in sun-shine and through tears;

All change to joy, my way with Thee be bright;
Fear - ing for naught, but trust-ing Thee in all,
My hand in Thine, though dark-ened be the way,

Van - ished at last the shad-ows of the night.
Thou wilt be near to help me lest I fall.
Still guide me on till dawns the per - fect day.

AN EVENING PRAYER

C. M. BATTERSBY
Arr. by C. H. G.

Copyright, 1911, by Chas. H. Gabriel
Homer Rodeheaver, owner

CHAS. H. GABRIEL

1. If I have wounded an-y soul to-day, If I have caused one foot to
2. If I have ut-tered i-dle words or vain, If I have turned a-side from
3. If I have been perverse or hard, or cold, If I have longed for shel-ter
4. Forgive the sins I have confessed to Thee; Forgive the se-cret sins I

go astray, If I have walked in my own will-ful way, Dear Lord, for-give!
want or pain, Lest I my-self shall suffer thro' the strain, Dear Lord, for-give!
in Thy fold, When Thou hast given me some fort to hold, Dear Lord, for-give!
do not see; O guide me, love me, and my keep-er be, A-men.

MY FAITH LOOKS UP TO THEE

RAY PALMER

LOWELL MASON

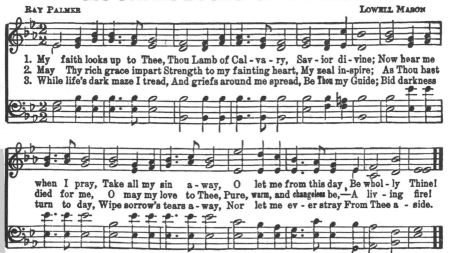

1. My faith looks up to Thee, Thou Lamb of Cal-va-ry, Sav-ior di-vine; Now hear me
2. May Thy rich grace impart Strength to my fainting heart, My zeal in-spire; As Thou hast
3. While life's dark maze I tread, And griefs around me spread, Be Thou my Guide; Bid darkness

when I pray, Take all my sin a-way, O let me from this day Be whol-ly Thine!
died for me, O may my love to Thee, Pure, warm, and changeless be,—A liv-ing fire!
turn to day, Wipe sorrow's tears a-way, Nor let me ev-er stray From Thee a-side.

I NEED THEE EVERY HOUR

MRS. ANNIE S. HAWKS

REV. ROBERT LOWRY

1. I need Thee ev-'ry hour, Most gra-cious Lord; No ten-der voice like
2. I need Thee ev-'ry hour, Stay Thou near by; Temp-ta-tions lose their
3. I need Thee ev-'ry hour, In joy or pain; Come quick-ly and a-
4. I need Thee ev-'ry hour, Most Ho-ly One; O make me Thine in-

CHORUS

Thine Can peace af-ford.
pow'r When Thou art nigh.
bide, Or life is vain.
deed, Thou bless-ed Son!

I need Thee, O I need Thee; Ev-'ry hour I

need Thee! O bless me now, my Sav-ior, I come to Thee!

107

JESUS SHALL REIGN

ISAAC WATTS

JOHN HATTON

1. Je-sus shall reign wher-e'er the sun Does his suc-ces-sive jour-neys run;
2. From north to south the prin-ces meet To pay their homage at His feet;
3. To Him shall end-less pray'r be made, And endless praises crown His head;
4. Peo-ple and realms of ev-'ry tongue Dwell on His love with sweetest song,

His kingdom spread from shore to shore, Till moons shall wax and wane no more.
While western em-pires own their Lord, And sav-age tribes at-tend His word.
His name like sweet per-fume shall rise With ev-'ry morn-ing sac-ri-fice.
And in-fant voic-es shall pro-claim Their earthly blessings on His name.

SAVIOR, MORE THAN LIFE

FANNY J. CROSBY

W. H. DOANE

1. Sav - ior, more than life to me, I am clinging, clinging close to Thee;
2. Thro' this changing world be - low, Lead me gen-tly, gen-tly as I go;
3. Let me love Thee more and more, Till this fleeting, fleeting life is o'er,

Let Thy pre-cious blood ap-plied; Keep me ev - er, ev - er near Thy side.
Trusting Thee, I can-not stray, I can nev-er, nev-er lose my way.
Till my soul is lost in love, In a brighter, brighter world a - bove.

D. S.—May Thy ten - der love to me Bind me clos-er, clos-er, Lord, to Thee.

REFRAIN

Ev-'ry day, ev-'ry hour, Let me feel Thy cleansing pow'r;
Ev - 'ry day and hour, Ev - 'ry day and hour,

109 SWEET PEACE, THE GIFT OF GOD'S LOVE

I AM THINE, O LORD

Fanny J. Crosby

W. H. Doane

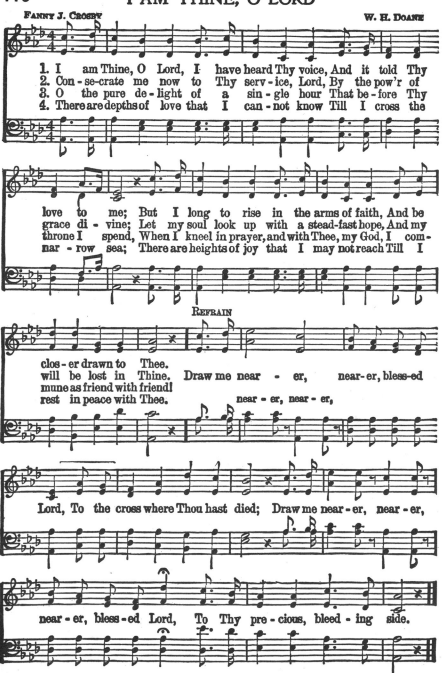

1. I am Thine, O Lord, I have heard Thy voice, And it told Thy love to me; But I long to rise in the arms of faith, And be clos-er drawn to Thee.
2. Con-se-crate me now to Thy serv-ice, Lord, By the pow'r of grace di-vine; Let my soul look up with a stead-fast hope, And my will be lost in Thine.
3. O the pure de-light of a sin-gle hour That be-fore Thy throne I spend, When I kneel in prayer, and with Thee, my God, I com-mune as friend with friend!
4. There are depths of love that I can-not know Till I cross the nar-row sea; There are heights of joy that I may not reach Till I rest in peace with Thee.

Refrain

Draw me near-er, near-er, bless-ed Lord, To the cross where Thou hast died; Draw me near-er, near-er, near-er, bless-ed Lord, To Thy pre-cious, bleed-ing side.

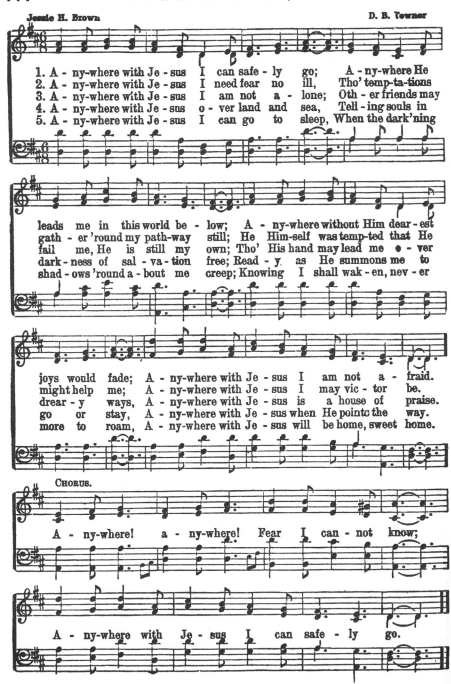

BLESSED ASSURANCE

FANNY J. CROSBY

MRS. JOS. F. KNAPP

1. Bless-ed as-sur-ance, Je-sus is mine! O what a fore-taste of
2. Per-fect sub-mis-sion, per-fect de-light, Vi-sions of rap-ture now
3. Per-fect sub-mis-sion, all is at rest, I in my Sav-ior am

glo-ry di-vine! Heir of sal-va-tion, purchase of God, Born of His
burst on my sight! Angels de-scend-ing, bring from a-bove Ech-oes of
hap-py and blest; Watching and waiting, look-ing a-bove, Filled with His

CHORUS

Spir-it, washed in His blood.
mer-cy, whis-pers of love.   This is my sto-ry, this is my
good-ness, lost in His love.

song, Prais-ing my Sav-ior all the day long; This is my

sto-ry, this is my song, Praising my Sav-ior all the day long.

MOMENT BY MOMENT

D. W. WHITTLE

MAY WHITTLE MOODY

1. Dy - ing with Je - sus, by death reckoned mine: Liv-ing with Je - sus, a
2. Nev - er a tri - al that He is not there, Nev-er a bur-den that
3. Nev - er a heartache, and nev - er a groan, Nev-er a teardrop and
4. Nev - er a weak-ness that He doth not feel, Nev-er a sickness that

new life di - vine; Looking to Je - sus till glo - ry doth shine, Mo-ment by
He doth not bear, Nev - er a sor-row that He doth not share, Mo-ment by
nev - er a moan; Nev - er a dan-ger but there on the throne, Mo-ment by
He can-not heal; Mo-ment by moment, in woe or in weal, Je - sus, my

CHORUS

mo-ment, O Lord, I am Thine.
mo-ment, I'm un - der His care. Moment by mo-ment I'm kept in His love;
mo-ment He thinks of His own.
Sav-ior, a-bides with me still.

Mo-ment by moment I've life from a - bove; Looking to Je - sus till

glo - ry doth shine; Mo-ment by mo - ment, O Lord, I am Thine.

By permission of Mrs. W. R. Moody, E. Northfield, Mass.

114 JESUS, I MY CROSS HAVE TAKEN

HENRY F. LYTE

From MOZART

1. Je - sus, I my cross have ta-ken, All to leave and fol-low Thee;
2. Let the world de-spise and leave me, They have left my Sav-ior, too;
3. Man may troub-le and dis-tress me, 'Twill but drive me to Thy breast;
4. Haste thee on from grace to glo-ry, Armed by faith and winged by pray'r;

Des - ti-tute, despised, for - sa-ken, Thou, from hence, my all shall be:
Hu - man hearts and looks de - ceive me; Thou art not, like man, un-true;
Life with tri - als hard may press me, Heav'n will bring me sweet-er rest.
Heav'n's e-ter - nal days be - fore thee, God's own hand shall guide thee there.

Per - ish ev - 'ry fond am - bi - tion, All I've sought, and hoped, and known;
And, while Thou shalt smile up - on me, God of wis - dom, love, and might,
O 'tis not in grief to harm me, While Thy love is left to me;
Soon shall close thy earth - ly mission, Swift shall pass thy pil - grim days,

Yet how rich is my con - di-tion, God and heav'n are still my own!
Foes may hate and friends may shun me; Show Thy face, and all is bright.
O 'twere not in joy to charm me, Were that joy unmixed with Thee.
Hope shall change to glad fru-i - tion, Faith to sight, and pray'r to praise. A-men.

115 FADE, FADE, EACH EARTHLY JOY

JANE C. BONAR   THEODORE E. PERKINS

1. Fade, fade, each earth-ly joy; Je - sus is mine. Break ev - 'ry
2. Tempt not my soul a - way; Je - sus is mine. Here would I
3. Fare - well, ye dreams of night; Je - sus is mine. Lost in this
4. Fare - well, mor - tal - i - ty; Je - sus is mine. Wel - come, e -

ten - der tie; Je - sus is mine. Dark is the wil - der-ness,
ev - er stay; Je - sus is mine. Per - ish - ing things of clay,
dawn-ing bright, Je - sus is mine. All that my soul has tried
ter - ni - ty; Je - sus is mine. Wel - come, O loved and blest,

Earth has no rest-ing-place, Je-sus a-lone can bless; Je - sus is mine.
Born but for one brief day, Pass from my heart a - way; Je - sus is mine.
Left but a dis-mal void; Je-sus has sat-is-fied; Je - sus is mine.
Welcome,sweet scenes of rest, Welcome,my Savior's breast; Je - sus is mine.

116 TAKE MY LIFE, AND LET IT BE

Frances R. Havergal   C. H. A. Malan

1. Take my life, and let it be Con-se-cra-ted, Lord, to Thee; Take my hands, and
2. Take my feet, and let them be Swift and beau-ti-ful for Thee; Take my voice, and
3. Take my sil - ver and my gold, Not a mite would I with-hold; Take my mo-ments
4. Take my will and make it Thine, It shall be no lon-ger mine; Take my heart, it

TAKE MY LIFE, AND LET IT BE

let them move At the im-pulse of Thy love, At the im-pulse of Thy love.
let me sing Al-ways, on - ly, for my King, Al-ways, on-ly, for my King.
and my days, Let them flow in cease-less praise, Let them flow in ceaseless praise.
is Thine own, It shall be Thy roy-al throne, It shall be Thy roy - al throne.

117   THE LIGHT OF THE WORLD IS JESUS

P. P. B.   P. P. Bliss

1. The whole world was lost in the darkness of sin; The Light of the world is Je-sus;
2. No darkness have we who in Je-sus a-bide; The Light of the world is Je-sus;
3. No dwellers in darkness with sin-blinded eyes; The Light of the world is Je-sus;
4. No need of the sunlight in heaven we're told; The Light of the world is Je-sus;

Like sunshine at noonday His glo-ry shone in, The Light of the world is Je-sus.
We walk in the Light when we follow our Guide, The Light of the world is Je-sus.
Go, wash at His bidding, and light will a-rise, The Light of the world is Je-sus.
The Lamb is the Light in the cit - y of gold, The Light of the world is Je-sus.

CHORUS.

Come to the Light, 'tis shining for thee; Sweetly the Light has dawned upon me,

Once I was blind, but now I can see: The Light of the world is Je - sus.

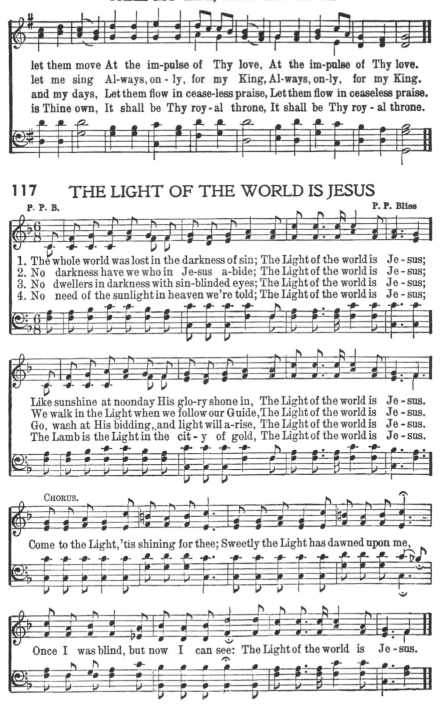

BENEATH THE CROSS OF JESUS

Elizabeth C. Clephane

Frederick C. Maker

1. Be-neath the cross of Je - sus I fain would take my stand,
2. Up - on that cross of Je - sus Mine eye at times can see
3. I take, O cross, thy shad - ow For my a - bid - ing place;

The shad - ow of a might-y rock With-in a wea - ry land;
The ver - y dy - ing form of One Who suf - fered there for me;
I ask no oth - er sun-shine than The sun - shine of His face;

A home with-in the wil - der - ness, A rest up-on the way,
And from my smit - ten heart with tears Two won - ders I con - fess,—
Con - tent to let the world go by, To know no gain or loss,

From the burning of the noon-tide heat, And the bur-den of the day.
The won - ders of His glo-rious love And my un-wor - thi - ness.
My sin - ful self my on - ly shame, My glo - ry all the cross.

HIGHER GROUND

Johnson Oatman, Jr.

Chas. H. Gabriel

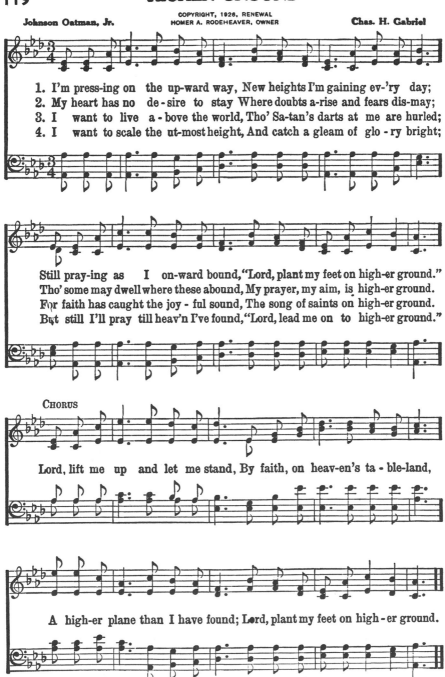

1. I'm press-ing on the up-ward way, New heights I'm gaining ev-'ry day;
2. My heart has no de-sire to stay Where doubts a-rise and fears dis-may;
3. I want to live a-bove the world, Tho' Sa-tan's darts at me are hurled;
4. I want to scale the ut-most height, And catch a gleam of glo-ry bright;

Still pray-ing as I on-ward bound, "Lord, plant my feet on high-er ground."
Tho' some may dwell where these abound, My prayer, my aim, is high-er ground.
For faith has caught the joy-ful sound, The song of saints on high-er ground.
But still I'll pray till heav'n I've found, "Lord, lead me on to high-er ground."

CHORUS

Lord, lift me up and let me stand, By faith, on heav-en's ta-ble-land,

A high-er plane than I have found; Lord, plant my feet on high-er ground.

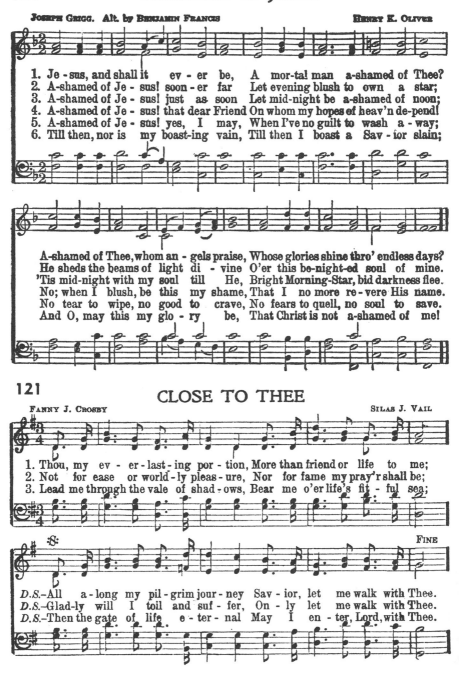

120

ASHAMED OF JESUS

Joseph Grigg. Alt. by Benjamin Francis · Henry K. Oliver

1. Je - sus, and shall it ev - er be, A mor - tal man a - shamed of Thee?
2. A - shamed of Je - sus! soon - er far Let evening blush to own a star;
3. A - shamed of Je - sus! just as soon Let mid-night be a - shamed of noon;
4. A - shamed of Je - sus! that dear Friend On whom my hopes of heav'n de - pend!
5. A - shamed of Je - sus! yes, I may, When I've no guilt to wash a - way;
6. Till then, nor is my boast-ing vain, Till then I boast a Sav - ior slain;

A - shamed of Thee, whom an - gels praise, Whose glories shine thro' endless days?
He sheds the beams of light di - vine O'er this be-night-ed soul of mine.
'Tis mid-night with my soul till He, Bright Morning-Star, bid darkness flee.
No; when I blush, be this my shame, That I no more re - vere His name.
No tear to wipe, no good to crave, No fears to quell, no soul to save.
And O, may this my glo - ry be, That Christ is not a - shamed of me!

121

CLOSE TO THEE

Fanny J. Crosby · Silas J. Vail

1. Thou, my ev - er - last - ing por - tion, More than friend or life to me;
2. Not for ease or world - ly pleas - ure, Nor for fame my pray'r shall be;
3. Lead me through the vale of shad - ows, Bear me o'er life's fit - ful sea;

FINE

D.S.—All a - long my pil - grim jour - ney Sav - ior, let me walk with Thee.
D.S.—Glad-ly will I toil and suf - fer, On - ly let me walk with Thee.
D.S.—Then the gate of life e - ter - nal May I en - ter, Lord, with Thee.

CLOSE TO THEE

REFRAIN

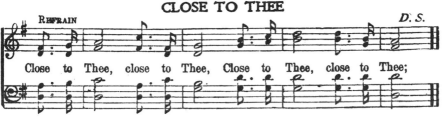

Close to Thee, close to Thee, Close to Thee, close to Thee;

122

HAVE THINE OWN WAY, LORD

A. A. P.

Geo. C. Stebbins

Slowly

1. Have Thine own way, Lord! Have Thine own way! Thou art the
2. Have Thine own way, Lord! Have Thine own way! Search me and
3. Have Thine own way, Lord! Have Thine own way! Wound-ed and
4. Have Thine own way, Lord! Have Thine own way! Hold o'er my

Pot - ter; I am the clay Mould me and make me Aft - er Thy
try me, Mas-ter, to - day! Whit - er than snow, Lord, Wash me just
wea - ry, Help me, I pray! Pow - er—all pow - er—Sure-ly is
be - ing Ab - so - lute sway! Fill with Thy Spir - it Till all shall

will, While I am wait - ing, Yield - ed and still.
now, As in Thy pres - ence Hum - bly I bow.
Thine! Touch me and heal me, Sav - ior di - vine!
see. Christ on - ly, al - ways, Liv - ing in me!

123 JESUS IS ALL THE WORLD TO ME

W. L. T.

Will L. Thompson

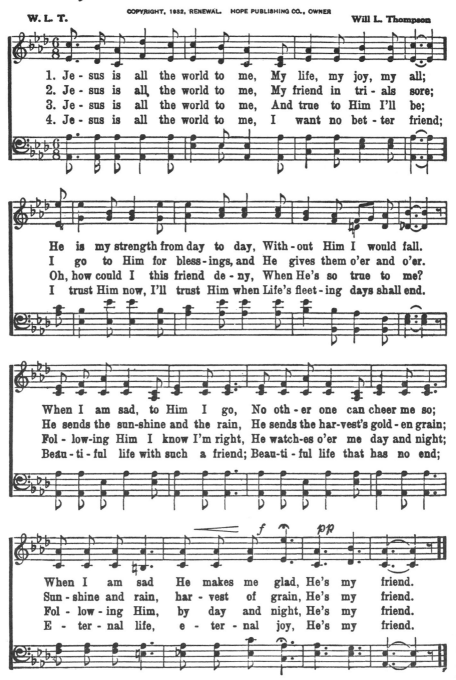

1. Je - sus is all the world to me, My life, my joy, my all;
2. Je - sus is all the world to me, My friend in tri - als sore;
3. Je - sus is all the world to me, And true to Him I'll be;
4. Je - sus is all the world to me, I want no bet - ter friend;

He is my strength from day to day, With - out Him I would fall.
I go to Him for bless - ings, and He gives them o'er and o'er.
Oh, how could I this friend de - ny, When He's so true to me?
I trust Him now, I'll trust Him when Life's fleet - ing days shall end.

When I am sad, to Him I go, No oth - er one can cheer me so;
He sends the sun-shine and the rain, He sends the har-vest's gold - en grain;
Fol - low-ing Him I know I'm right, He watch-es o'er me day and night;
Beau - ti - ful life with such a friend; Beau - ti - ful life that has no end;

When I am sad He makes me glad, He's my friend.
Sun - shine and rain, har - vest of grain, He's my friend.
Fol - low - ing Him, by day and night, He's my friend.
E - ter - nal life, e - ter - nal joy, He's my friend.

124 SAVIOR, LIKE A SHEPHERD LEAD US

DOROTHY ANN THRUPP

WILLIAM B. BRADBURY

1. Sav - ior, like a Shep-herd lead us, Much we need Thy ten-der care;
2. We are Thine, do Thou be - friend us, Be the Guardian of our way;
3. Thou hast promised to re - ceive us, Poor and sin-ful tho' we be;
4. Ear - ly let us seek Thy fa - vor; Ear - ly let us seek Thy will;

In Thy pleasant pas-tures feed us, For our use Thy folds pre-pare:
Keep Thy flock, from sin de - fend us, Seek us when we go a - stray:
Thou hast mer - cy to re - lieve us, Grace to cleanse, and pow'r to free:
Bless - ed Lord and on - ly Sav - ior, With Thy love our bos-oms fill:

Bless-ed Je - sus, Bless-ed Je - sus, Thou hast bought us, Thine we are;
Bless-ed Je - sus, Bless-ed Je - sus, Hear Thy chil - dren when they pray;
Bless-ed Je - sus, Bless-ed Je - sus, Ear - ly let us turn to Thee;
Bless-ed Je - sus, Bless-ed Je - sus, Thou hast loved us, love us still;

Bless-ed Je - sus, Bless-ed Je - sus, Thou hast bought us, Thine we are.
Bless-ed Je - sus, Bless-ed Je - sus, Hear Thy children when they pray.
Bless-ed Je - sus, Bless-ed Je - sus, Ear - ly let us turn to Thee.
Bless-ed Je - sus, Bless-ed Je - sus, Thou hast loved us, love us still.

125 GUIDE ME, O THOU GREAT JEHOVAH

WILLIAM WILLIAMS   CWM RHONDDA   JOHN HUGHES

1. Guide me, O Thou great Je - ho - vah, Pil-grim through this bar-ren land;
2. O - pen now the crys-tal fountain Whence the heal - ing wa - ters flow;
3. When I tread the verge of Jor - dan, Bid my anx - ious fears sub-side;

I am weak, but Thou art might-y, Hold me with Thy pow'r-ful hand;
Let the fi - er-y, cloud-y pil - lar Lead me all my jour-ney thro';
Bear me thro' the swell-ing cur - rent, Land me safe on Ca-naan's side:

Bread of heav - en, Bread of heav - en, Feed me till I want no
Strong De-liv -'rer, Strong De-liv -'rer, Be Thou still my Strength and
Songs of prais-es, Songs of prais - es I will ev-er give to

more, (no more,) Feed me till I want no more.
Shield, (and Shield,) Be Thou still my Strength and Shield.
Thee, (to Thee,) I will ev - er give to Thee. A - men.

By permission Mrs. John Hughes, Tregarth, Tonteg, Pontypridd, Glam.

SABINE BARING-GOULD

ARTHUR SULLIVAN

1. On-ward, Christian sol - diers! Marching as to war, With the cross of
2. Like a might-y ar - my Moves the Church of God; Brothers, we are
3. Crowns and thrones may perish, Kingdoms rise and wane; But the Church of
4. On-ward, then, ye peo - ple! Join our happy throng; Blend with ours your

Je - sus Go - ing on be - fore; Christ, the roy - al Mas - ter,
tread - ing Where the saints have trod; We are not di - vid - ed,
Je - sus Con-stant will re - main; Gates of hell can nev - er
voic - es In the tri-umph song; Glo - ry, laud, and hon - or,

Leads a-gainst the foe; For-ward in - to bat - tle, See, His banners go!
All one bod - y we; One in hope and doc - trine, One in char - i - ty.
'Gainst that Church prevail; We have Christ's own promise, Which can never fail.
Un - to Christ the King; This thro' countless a - ges Men and an - gels sing.

CHORUS

On-ward, Chris-tian sol - diers! March-ing as to war,

With the cross of Je - sus Go - ing on be - fore.

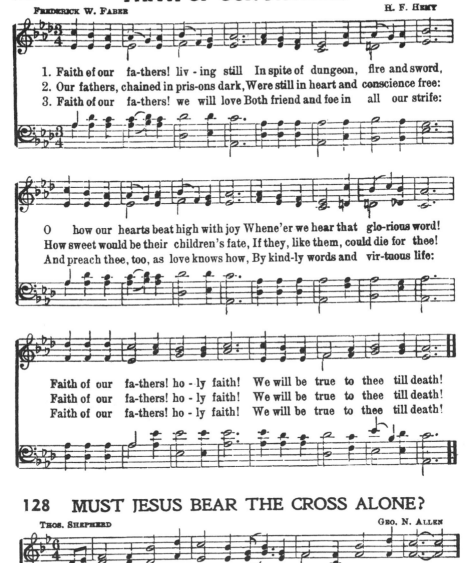

127 FAITH OF OUR FATHERS

Frederick W. Faber

H. F. Hemy

1. Faith of our fa-thers! liv-ing still In spite of dungeon, fire and sword,
2. Our fathers, chained in pris-ons dark, Were still in heart and conscience free:
3. Faith of our fa-thers! we will love Both friend and foe in all our strife:

O how our hearts beat high with joy Whene'er we hear that glo-rious word!
How sweet would be their children's fate, If they, like them, could die for thee!
And preach thee, too, as love knows how, By kind-ly words and vir-tuous life:

Faith of our fa-thers! ho-ly faith! We will be true to thee till death!
Faith of our fa-thers! ho-ly faith! We will be true to thee till death!
Faith of our fa-thers! ho-ly faith! We will be true to thee till death!

128 MUST JESUS BEAR THE CROSS ALONE?

Thos. Shepherd

Geo. N. Allen

1. Must Je-sus bear the cross a-lone, And all the world go free?
2. How hap-py are the saints a-bove, Who once went sor-rowing here!
3. The con-se-cra-ted cross I'll bear, Till death shall set me free;
4. Up-on the crys-tal pavement, down, At Je-sus' pierc-ed feet,

MUST JESUS BEAR THE CROSS ALONE?

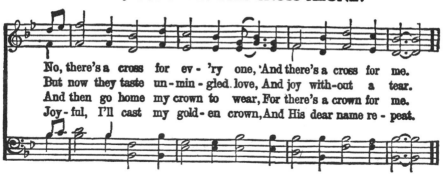

No, there's a cross for ev - 'ry one, 'And there's a cross for me.
But now they taste un - min - gled. love, And joy with-out a tear.
And then go home my crown to wear, For there's a crown for me.
Joy - ful, I'll cast my gold- en crown, And His dear name re - peat.

129   JESUS LOVES EVEN ME

P. P. B.

P. P. BLISS

1. I am so glad that our Father in heav'n Tells of His love in the Book He has giv'n;
2. Tho' I for - get Him and wander away, Kind-ly He follows wherev - er I stray;
3. Oh, if there's on-ly one song I can sing, When in His beauty I see the great King,

Won-der-ful things in the Bi - ble I see, This is the dearest, that Jesus loves me.
Back to His dear lov-ing arms would I flee, When I re-member that Jesus loves me.
This shall my song in e - ter - ni - ty be, Oh, what a wonder that Jesus loves me!

REFRAIN

I am so glad that Je-sus loves me, Je - sus loves me, Je - sus loves me,

I am so glad that Je - sus loves me, Je - sus loves e ven me.

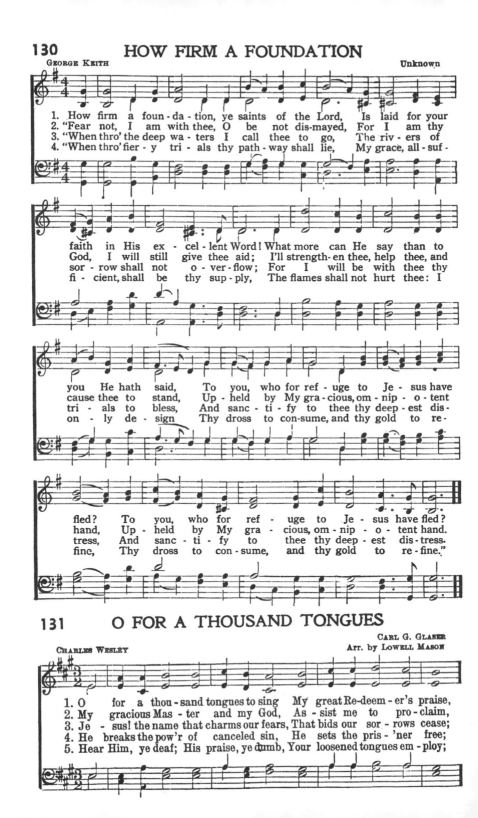

130   HOW FIRM A FOUNDATION

GEORGE KEITH

Unknown

1. How firm a foun-da-tion, ye saints of the Lord, Is laid for your
2. "Fear not, I am with thee, O be not dis-mayed, For I am thy
3. "When thro' the deep wa-ters I call thee to go, The riv-ers of
4. "When thro' fier-y tri-als thy path-way shall lie, My grace, all-suf-

faith in His ex-cel-lent Word! What more can He say than to
God, I will still give thee aid; I'll strength-en thee, help thee, and
sor-row shall not o-ver-flow; For I will be with thee thy
fi-cient, shall be thy sup-ply, The flames shall not hurt thee: I

you He hath said, To you, who for ref-uge to Je-sus have
cause thee to stand, Up-held by My gra-cious, om-nip-o-tent
tri-als to bless, And sanc-ti-fy to thee thy deep-est dis-
on-ly de-sign Thy dross to con-sume, and thy gold to re-

fled? To you, who for ref-uge to Je-sus have fled?
hand, Up-held by My gra-cious, om-nip-o-tent hand.
tress, And sanc-ti-fy to thee thy deep-est dis-tress.
fine, Thy dross to con-sume, and thy gold to re-fine."

131   O FOR A THOUSAND TONGUES

CARL G. GLASER
ARR. by LOWELL MASON

CHARLES WESLEY

1. O for a thou-sand tongues to sing My great Re-deem-er's praise,
2. My gracious Mas-ter and my God, As-sist me to pro-claim,
3. Je-sus! the name that charms our fears, That bids our sor-rows cease;
4. He breaks the pow'r of canceled sin, He sets the pris-'ner free;
5. Hear Him, ye deaf; His praise, ye dumb, Your loosened tongues em-ploy;

O FOR A THOUSAND TONGUES

The glo-ries of my God and King, The triumphs of His grace.
To spread thro' all the earth a-broad The hon-ors of Thy name.
'Tis mu-sic in the sin-ner's ears, 'Tis life, and health, and peace.
His blood can make the foul-est clean; His blood a-vailed for me.
Ye blind, be-hold your Sav-ior come; And leap, ye lame, for joy.

132

I'LL BE A SUNBEAM

To my grandson, Edwin O. Excell, Jr.

NELLIE TALBOT   Copyright, 1928, by E. O. Excell. Words and music   E. O. EXCELL

1. Je-sus wants me for a sun-beam, To shine for Him each day;......
2. Je-sus wants me to be lov-ing, And kind to all I see;......
3. I will ask Je-sus to help me To keep my heart from sin;......
4. I'll be a sun-beam for Je-sus; I can if I but try;......

In ev-'ry way try to please Him, At home, at school, at play......
Show-ing how pleas-ant and hap-py His lit-tle one can be.........
Ev-er re-flect-ing His good-ness, And al-ways shine for Him......
Serv-ing Him mo-ment by mo-ment, Then live with Him on high......

CHORUS

A sun-beam, a sun-beam, Je-sus wants me for a sun-beam;

A sun-beam, a sun-beam, I'll be a sun-beam for Him.

133 COUNT YOUR BLESSINGS

REV. J. OATMAN, JR.

E. O. EXCELL

1. When up-on life's bil-lows you are tem-pest-tossed,When you are dis-
2. Are you ev- er burdened with a load of care? Does the cross seem
3. When you look at oth-ers with their lands and gold, Think that Christ has
4. So, a-mid the con-flict,whether great or small, Do not be dis-

couraged,thinking all is - lost, Count your many blessings,name them one by
heav-y you are called to bear?Count your many blessings,ev-'ry doubt will
promised you His wealth un - told;Count your many blessings,money can not
couraged,God is o - ver all; Count your many blessings,angels will at -

CHORUS

one, And it will sur-prise you what the Lord hath done.
fly, And you will be sing-ing as the days go by. Count your blessings,Name them
buy Your re-ward in heaven, nor your home on high.
tend,Help and comfort give you to your journey's end.

Count your many blessings,

one by one; Count your blessings,See what God hath done;Count your
Name them one by one;Count your many blessings, See what God hath done;Count your ma

COUNT YOUR BLESSINGS

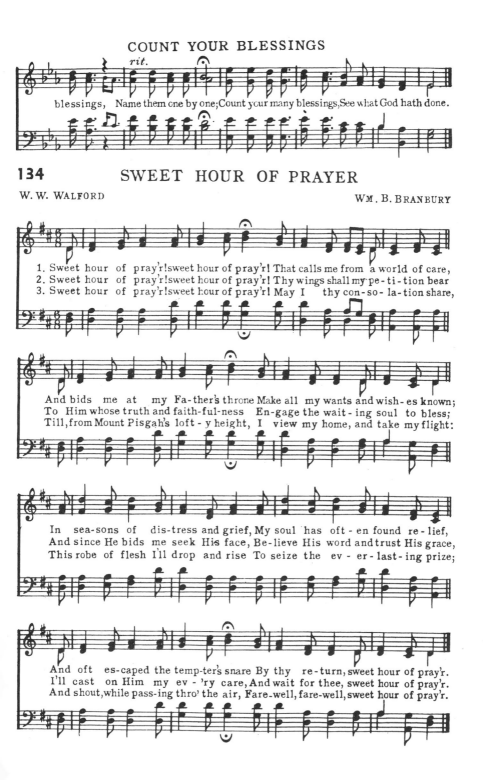

blessings, Name them one by one; Count your many blessings, See what God hath done.

134   # SWEET HOUR OF PRAYER

W. W. WALFORD

WM. B. BRANBURY

1. Sweet hour of pray'r! sweet hour of pray'r! That calls me from a world of care,
2. Sweet hour of pray'r! sweet hour of pray'r! Thy wings shall my pe-ti-tion bear
3. Sweet hour of pray'r! sweet hour of pray'r! May I thy con-so-la-tion share,

And bids me at my Fa-ther's throne Make all my wants and wish-es known;
To Him whose truth and faith-ful-ness En-gage the wait-ing soul to bless;
Till, from Mount Pisgah's loft-y height, I view my home, and take my flight:

In sea-sons of dis-tress and grief, My soul has oft-en found re-lief,
And since He bids me seek His face, Be-lieve His word and trust His grace,
This robe of flesh I'll drop and rise To seize the ev-er-last-ing prize;

And oft es-caped the temp-ter's snare By thy re-turn, sweet hour of pray'r.
I'll cast on Him my ev-'ry care, And wait for thee, sweet hour of pray'r.
And shout, while pass-ing thro' the air, Fare-well, fare-well, sweet hour of pray'r.

135 TRUST AND OBEY

J. H. SAMMIS

D. B. TOWNER

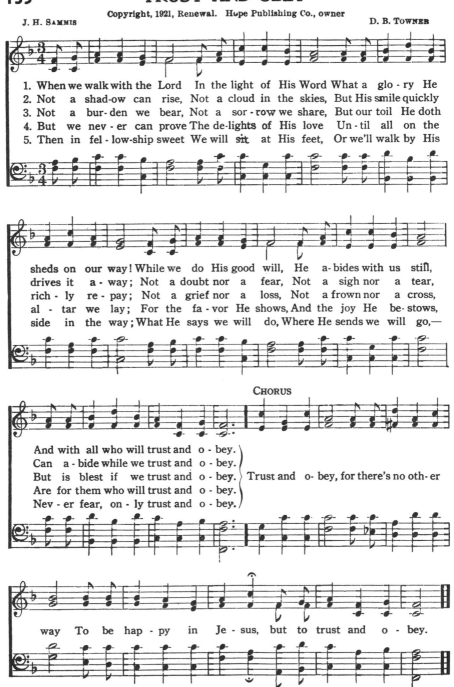

1. When we walk with the Lord In the light of His Word What a glo-ry He
2. Not a shad-ow can rise, Not a cloud in the skies, But His smile quickly
3. Not a bur-den we bear, Not a sor-row we share, But our toil He doth
4. But we nev-er can prove The de-lights of His love Un-til all on the
5. Then in fel-low-ship sweet We will sit at His feet, Or we'll walk by His

sheds on our way! While we do His good will, He a-bides with us still,
drives it a-way; Not a doubt nor a fear, Not a sigh nor a tear,
rich-ly re-pay; Not a grief nor a loss, Not a frown nor a cross,
al-tar we lay; For the fa-vor He shows, And the joy He be-stows,
side in the way; What He says we will do, Where He sends we will go,—

CHORUS

And with all who will trust and o-bey.
Can a-bide while we trust and o-bey.
But is blest if we trust and o-bey.   Trust and o-bey, for there's no oth-er
Are for them who will trust and o-bey.
Nev-er fear, on-ly trust and o-bey.

way To be hap-py in Je-sus, but to trust and o-bey.

JESUS, I COME

W. T. Sleeper

Geo. C. Stebbins

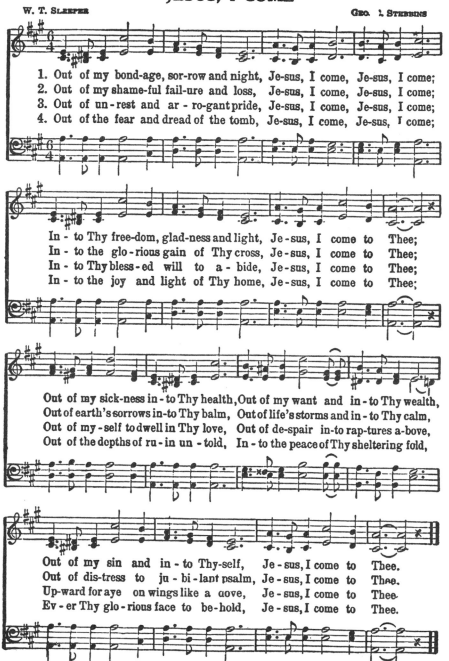

1. Out of my bond-age, sor-row and night, Je-sus, I come, Je-sus, I come;
2. Out of my shame-ful fail-ure and loss, Je-sus, I come, Je-sus, I come;
3. Out of un-rest and ar-ro-gant pride, Je-sus, I come, Je-sus, I come;
4. Out of the fear and dread of the tomb, Je-sus, I come, Je-sus, I come;

In-to Thy free-dom, glad-ness and light, Je-sus, I come to Thee;
In-to the glo-rious gain of Thy cross, Je-sus, I come to Thee;
In-to Thy bless-ed will to a-bide, Je-sus, I come to Thee;
In-to the joy and light of Thy home, Je-sus, I come to Thee;

Out of my sick-ness in-to Thy health, Out of my want and in-to Thy wealth,
Out of earth's sorrows in-to Thy balm, Out of life's storms and in-to Thy calm,
Out of my-self to dwell in Thy love, Out of de-spair in-to rap-tures a-bove,
Out of the depths of ru-in un-told, In-to the peace of Thy sheltering fold,

Out of my sin and in-to Thy-self, Je-sus, I come to Thee.
Out of dis-tress to ju-bi-lant psalm, Je-sus, I come to Thee.
Up-ward for aye on wings like a dove, Je-sus, I come to Thee.
Ev-er Thy glo-rious face to be-hold, Je-sus, I come to Thee.

137 WHEN THE MISTS HAVE ROLLED AWAY

ANNIE HERBERT. Arr   IRA D. SANKEY

1. When the mists have rolled in splendor From the beau-ty of the hills, And the
2. Oft we tread the path be-fore us With a wea-ry, burdened heart; Oft we
3. We shall come with joy and gladness, We shall gath-er round the throne; Face to

sun-light falls in glad-ness On the riv-er and the rills, We re-call our
toil a-mid the shadows, And our fields are far a-part; But the Sav-iour's
face with those that love us, We shall know as we are known: And the song of

Fa-ther's prom-ise In the rain-bow of the spray: We shall know each oth-er
"Come, ye blessed" All our la-bor will re-pay, When we gath-er in the
our re-demp-tion Shall re-sound thro' end-less day When the shad-ows have de-

rit.   CHORUS

bet-ter When the mists have rolled a-way. } We shall know...... as we are
morning Where the mists have rolled a-way. }
part-ed, And the mists have rolled a-way. }   We shall know

known,........... Nev-er-more......... to walk a-lone,...............
as we are known,   Nev-er-more   to walk a-lone,

WHEN THE MISTS HAVE ROLLED AWAY

In the dawn-ing of the morn-ing Of that bright and hap-py day,

We shall know each oth-er bet-ter When the mists have rolled a-way.

138 PRAYER OF THANKSGIVING

Arrangement Copyright, 1928, by Homer A. Rodeheaver

E. KREMSOR
Arr. by C. H. G.

1. We ga-ther to-geth-er to ask the Lord's bless-ing, He chas-tens and
2. Be-side us to guide us, our God with us join-ing, Or-dain-ing, main-
3. We all do ex-tol Thee, Thou Lead-er in bat-tle, And pray that Thou

has-tens His will to make known; The wick-ed op-press-ing, cease
tain-ing His king-dom di-vine, So from the be-gin-ning the
still our De-fend-er wilt be. Let Thy con-gre-ga-tion es-

them from dis-tress-ing, Sing praises to His name, He for-gets not His own.
fight we were win-ning; Thou, Lord, wast at our side, all glo-ry be Thine!
cape trib-u-la-tion! Thy name be ev-er praised! O Lord, make us free.

HARK, HARK, MY SOUL!

CHOIR OR QUARTET.

F. W. Faber. Geo. H. Crosby.

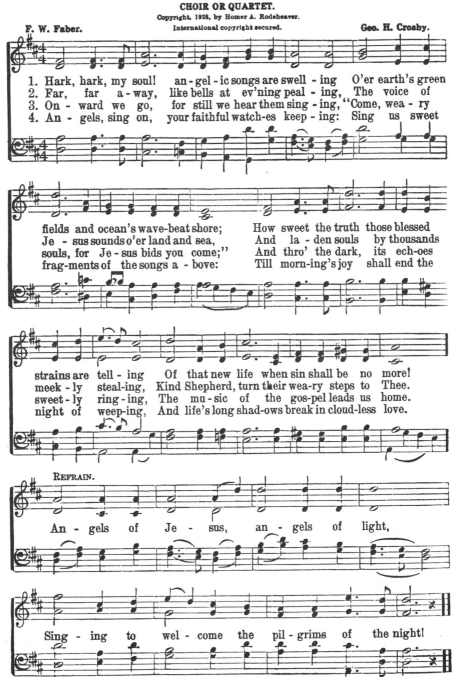

1. Hark, hark, my soul! an-gel-ic songs are swell-ing O'er earth's green fields and ocean's wave-beat shore; How sweet the truth those blessed strains are tell-ing Of that new life when sin shall be no more!

2. Far, far a-way, like bells at ev'ning peal-ing, The voice of Je-sus sounds o'er land and sea, And la-den souls by thousands meek-ly steal-ing, Kind Shepherd, turn their wea-ry steps to Thee.

3. On-ward we go, for still we hear them sing-ing, "Come, wea-ry souls, for Je-sus bids you come;" And thro' the dark, its ech-oes sweet-ly ring-ing, The mu-sic of the gos-pel leads us home.

4. An-gels, sing on, your faithful watch-es keep-ing: Sing us sweet frag-ments of the songs a-bove: Till morn-ing's joy shall end the night of weep-ing, And life's long shad-ows break in cloud-less love.

REFRAIN.

An-gels of Je-sus, an-gels of light,

Sing-ing to wel-come the pil-grims of the night!

140 WATCHMAN, TELL US OF THE NIGHT

JOHN BOWRING

LOWELL MASON

1. Watchman, tell us of the night, What its signs of promise are; Trav'ler, o'er yon mountain's
2. Watchman, tell us of the night; High-er yet the star ascends; Trav'ler, bless-ed-ness and
3. Watchman, tell us of the night, For the morning seems to dawn; Trav'ler, darkness takes its

height See that glo - ry-beam-ing star! Watchman, does its beauteous ray Aught of hope or
light, Peace and truth its course portends; Watchman, will its beams alone Gild the spot that
flight; Doubt and ter-ror are withdrawn; Watchman, let thy wand'ring cease, Hie thee to thy

joy foretell? Trav-'ler, yes; it brings the day, Promised day of Is - ra - el.
gave them birth? Trav'ler a - ges are its own, See, it bursts o'er all the earth.
qui - et home! Trav'ler, lo, the Prince of Peace, Lo, the Son of God is come! A - men.

141 MAJESTIC SWEETNESS SITS ENTHRONED

Samuel Stennett

ORTONVILLE C. M.

Thomas Hastings

1. Majestic sweetness sits enthroned Upon the Saviour's brow; His head with radiant
2. He saw me plunged in deep distress, He flew to my relief; For me He bore the
3. To Him I owe my life and breath, And all the joys I have; He makes me triumph
4. To heav'n, the place of His abode, He brings my weary feet; Shows me the glories
5. Since from His bounty I receive Such proofs of love divine, Had I a thousand

glories crowned, His lips with grace o'erflow, His lips with grace o'erflow.
shameful cross, And carried all my grief, And carried all my grief.
o - ver death, He saves me from the grave, He saves me from the grave.
of my God, And makes my joys complete, And makes my joys complete.
hearts to give, Lord, they should all be Thine, Lord, they should all be Thine. A - men.

142   O JESUS, I HAVE PROMISED

JOHN E. BODE

ARTHUR H. MANN

1. O Je-sus, I have promised To serve Thee to the end; Be Thou for-ev - er
2. O let me feel Thee near me, The world is ev - er near; I see the sights that
3. O Jesus, Thou hast promised To all who fol-low Thee That where Thou art in

near me, My Mas-ter and my Friend: I shall not fear the bat - tle If Thou art
dazzle, The tempting sounds I hear: My foes are ev - er near me, Around me
glo - ry There shall Thy servant be; And, Je - sus, I have promised To serve Thee

by my side, Nor wan-der from the path - way If Thou wilt be my Guide.
and with - in; But, Je - sus, draw Thou nearer, And shield my soul from sin.
to the end; O give me grace to fol - low My Mas - ter and my Friend.

143   WHERE HE LEADS ME

E. W. Blandly

J. S. Norris

1. I can hear my Sav - ior call-ing, I can hear my Sav - ior call-ing,
2. I'll go with Him thro' the gar-den, I'll go with Him thro' the gar-den,
3. I'll go with Him thro' the judg-ment, I'll go with Him thro' the judg-ment,
4. He will give me grace and glo - ry, He will give me grace and glo - ry,

REF.—*Where He leads me I will fol - low, Where He leads me I will fol - low*

WHERE HE LEADS ME

I can hear my Sav-ior call-ing, "Take thy cross and fol-low, fol - low Me."
I'll go with Him thro' the gar-den, I'll go with Him, with Him all the way.
I'll go with Him thr.' the judg-ment, I'll go with Him, with Him all the way.
He will give me grace and glo - ry, And go with me, with me all the way.

Where He leads me I will fol - low, I'll go with Him, with Him all the way.

144   COME, THOU ALMIGHTY KING

ANONYMOUS   FELICE DE GIARDINI

1. Come, Thou Al - might - y King,   Help us Thy name to sing,
2. Come, Thou In - car - nate Word,   Gird on Thy might - y sword,
3. Come, Ho - ly Com - fort - er,   Thy sa - cred wit - ness bear
4. To the great One in Three   E - ter - nal prais - es be

Help us to praise: Fa - ther, all - glo - ri - ous, O'er all vic -
Our pray'r at - tend: Come, and Thy peo - ple bless, And give Thy
In this glad hour: Thou who al - might - y art,   Now rule in
Hence ev - er - more, His sov-'reign maj - es - ty   May we in

to - ri - ous, Come, and reign o - ver us, An - cient of Days.
word suc - cess: Spir - it of ho - li - ness, On us de - scend.
ev - 'ry heart, And ne'er from us de - part, Spir - it of pow'r.
glo - ry see, And to e - ter - ni - ty, Love and a - dore.

MY JESUS, I LOVE THEE

ANONYMOUS

A. J. GORDON

1. My Je-sus, I love Thee, I know Thou art mine, For Thee all the
2. I'll love Thee in life, I will love Thee in death, And praise Thee as
3. In mansions of glo-ry and end-less de-light, I'll ev-er a-

pleas-ures of sin I re-sign; My gra-cious Re-deem-er, my
long as Thou lend-est me breath; And say when the death-dew lies
dore Thee in heav-en so bright; I'll sing with the glit-ter-ing

Sav-ior art Thou; If ev-er I loved Thee, my Je-sus, 'tis now.
cold on my brow, If ev-er I loved Thee, my Je-sus, 'tis now.
crown on my brow, If ev-er I loved Thee, my Je-sus, 'tis now.

JESUS, SAVIOR, PILOT ME

Edward Hopper

J. E. Gould
FINE.

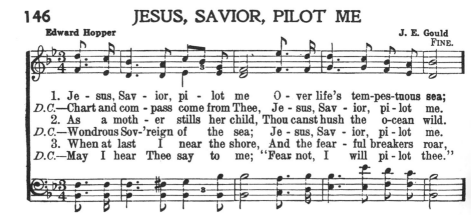

1. Je-sus, Sav-ior, pi-lot me O-ver life's tem-pes-tuous sea;
D.C.—Chart and com-pass come from Thee, Je-sus, Sav-ior, pi-lot me.
2. As a moth-er stills her child, Thou canst hush the o-cean wild.
D.C.—Wondrous Sov-'reign of the sea; Je-sus, Sav-ior, pi-lot me.
3. When at last I near the shore, And the fear-ful breakers roar,
D.C.—May I hear Thee say to me; "Fear not, I will pi-lot thee."

JESUS, SAVIOR, PILOT ME

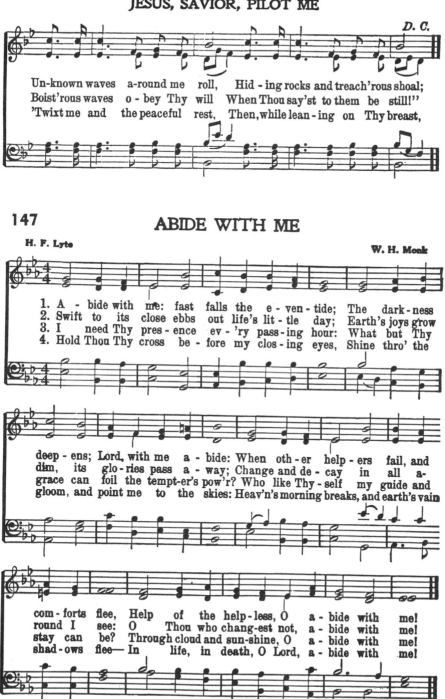

D. C.

Un-known waves a-round me roll, Hid - ing rocks and treach'rous shoal;
Boist'rous waves o - bey Thy will When Thou say'st to them be still!"
'Twixt me and the peaceful rest, Then, while lean - ing on Thy breast,

147

ABIDE WITH ME

H. F. Lyte

W. H. Monk

1. A - bide with me: fast falls the e - ven - tide; The dark - ness
2. Swift to its close ebbs out life's lit - tle day; Earth's joys grow
3. I need Thy pres - ence ev - 'ry pass-ing hour: What but Thy
4. Hold Thou Thy cross be - fore my clos - ing eyes, Shine thro' the

deep - ens; Lord, with me a - bide: When oth - er help - ers fail, and
dim, its glo-ries pass a - way; Change and de - cay in all a -
grace can foil the tempt-er's pow'r? Who like Thy - self my guide and
gloom, and point me to the skies: Heav'n's morning breaks, and earth's vain

com - forts flee, Help of the help-less, O a - bide with me!
round I see: O Thou who chang-est not, a - bide with me!
stay can be? Through cloud and sun-shine, O a - bide with me!
shad - ows flee— In life, in death, O Lord, a - bide with me!

148 HE IS LOVE

ANON

Arr. by HUBERT P. MAIN

1. Love Him, love Him, all ye lit - tle children, He is love, He is love,
2. Thank Him, thank Him, all ye lit - tle children, He is love, He is love,
3. Serve Him, serve Him, all ye lit - tle children, He is love, He is love,

Love Him, love Him, all ye lit - tle children, He is love, He is love.
Thank Him, thank Him, all ye lit - tle children, He is love, He is love.
Serve Him, serve Him, all ye lit - tle children, He is love, He is love.

149 BREAK THOU THE BREAD OF LIFE

MARY ANN LATHBURY

WILLIAM F. SHERWIN

1. Break Thou the bread of life, Dear Lord, to me, As Thou didst
2. Bless Thou the Truth, dear Lord, To me— to me— As Thou didst
3. O send Thy Spir - it, Lord, Now un - to me, That He may
4. Thou art the bread of life, O Lord, to me, Thy ho - ly

break the loaves Be - side the sea; Be - yond the sa - cred page
bless the bread By Gal - li - lee; Then shall all bond - age cease,
touch my eyes, And make me see: Show me the truth con-cealed
Word the truth That sav - eth me; Give me to eat and live

I seek Thee, Lord; My spir - it pants for Thee, O Liv - ing Word.
All fet - ters fall; And I shall find my peace, My All in all.
With - in Thy Word, And in Thy book re-vealed I see the Lord.
With Theee a - bove; Teach me to love Thy truth, For Thou art love.

I WILL SING THE WONDROUS STORY

F. H. ROWLEY

PETER P. BILHORN

1. I will sing the won-drous sto - ry Of the Christ who died for me,
2. I was lost, but Je - sus found me, Found the sheep that went a - stray,
3. I was bruised, but Je - sus healed me; Faint was I from man-y a fall;
4. Days of dark-ness still come o'er me, Sor-row's paths I oft - en tread,
5. He will keep me till the riv - er Rolls its wa - ters at my feet;

How He left His home in glo - ry For the cross of Cal - va - ry.
Threw His lov - ing arms a - round me, Drew me back in - to His way.
Sight was gone, and fears pos-sessed me, But He freed me from them all.
But the Sav - iour still is with me; By His hand I'm safe - ly led.
Then He'll bear me safe - ly o - ver, Where the loved ones I shall meet.

CHORUS

Yes, I'll sing .... the won-drous sto - ry Of the
Yes, I'll sing the won-drous sto - ry

Christ .... who died for me, Sing it with .... the saints in
Of the Christ who died for me, Sing it with

glo - ry, Gath-ered by ...... the crys-tal sea ....
the saints in glo - ry, Gath-ered by the crystal sea.

151 'TIS MIDNIGHT; AND ON OLIVE'S BROW

William B. Tappan

William B. Bradbury

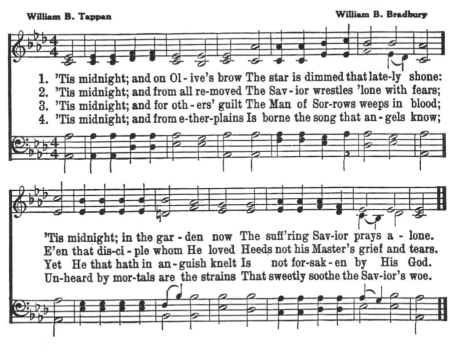

1. 'Tis midnight; and on Ol-ive's brow The star is dimmed that late-ly shone:
2. 'Tis midnight; and from all re-moved The Sav-ior wrestles 'lone with fears;
3. 'Tis midnight; and for oth-ers' guilt The Man of Sor-rows weeps in blood;
4. 'Tis midnight; and from e-ther-plains Is borne the song that an-gels know;

'Tis midnight; in the gar-den now The suff'ring Sav-ior prays a-lone.
E'en that dis-ci-ple whom He loved Heeds not his Master's grief and tears.
Yet He that hath in an-guish knelt Is not for-sak-en by His God.
Un-heard by mor-tals are the strains That sweetly soothe the Sav-ior's woe.

152 I GAVE MY LIFE FOR THEE

FRANCES R. HAVERGAL

P. P. Bliss

1. I gave My life for thee, My pre-cious blood I shed,
2. My Fa-ther's house of light, My glo-ry-cir-cled throne,
3. I suf-fered much for thee, More than thy tongue can tell,
4. And I have brought to thee, Down from My home a-bove,

That thou might'st ran-somed be, And quick-ened from the dead;
I left for earth-ly night, For wan-d'rings sad and lone;
Of bit-t'rest ag-o-ny, To res-cue thee from hell;
Sal-va-tion full and free, My par-don and My love;

I GAVE MY LIFE FOR THEE

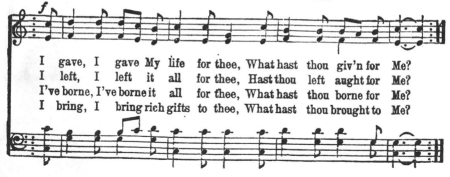

I gave, I gave My life for thee, What hast thou giv'n for Me?
I left, I left it all for thee, Hast thou left aught for Me?
I've borne, I've borne it all for thee, What hast thou borne for Me?
I bring, I bring rich gifts to thee, What hast thou brought to Me?

153   IN THE HOUR OF TRIAL

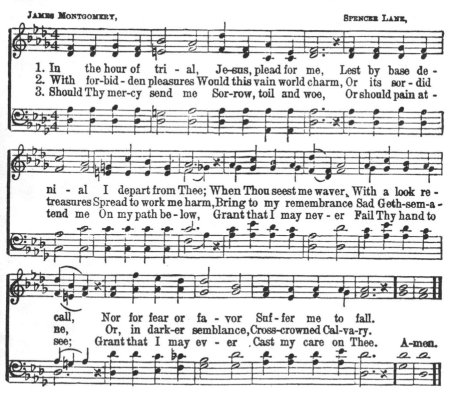

JAMES MONTGOMERY,

SPENCER LANE,

1. In the hour of tri - al, Je-sus, plead for me, Lest by base de -
2. With for-bid-den pleasures Would this vain world charm, Or its sor - did
3. Should Thy mer-cy send me Sor-row, toil and woe, Or should pain at -

ni - al I depart from Thee; When Thou seest me waver, With a look re-
treasures Spread to work me harm, Bring to my remembrance Sad Geth-sem-a-
tend me On my path be - low, Grant that I may nev - er Fail Thy hand to

call, Nor for fear or fa - vor Suf - fer me to fall.
ne, Or, in dark-er semblance, Cross-crowned Cal-va-ry.
see; Grant that I may ev - er Cast my care on Thee.   A-men.

154 MY HOPE IS BUILT

EDWARD MOTE

WILLIAM B. BRADBURY

1. My hope is built on noth-ing less Than Je-sus' blood and righteousness;
2. When darkness veils His love-ly face, I rest on His unchanging grace;
3. His oath, His cov-e-nant, His blood Sup-port me in the whelming flood;
4. When He shall come with trumpet sound, Oh, may I then in Him be found;

I dare not trust the sweetest frame, But whol-ly lean on Je-sus' name.
In ev-'ry high and storm-y gale, My an-chor holds with-in the veil.
When all a-round my soul gives way, He then is all my hope and stay.
Dressed in His right-eous-ness a-lone, Fault-less to stand be-fore the throne.

REFRAIN

On Christ, the sol-id Rock, I stand; All oth-er ground is

sink-ing sand, All oth-er ground is sink-ing sand. A-men.

155   HE LEADETH ME

Joseph H. Gilmore

William B. Bradbury

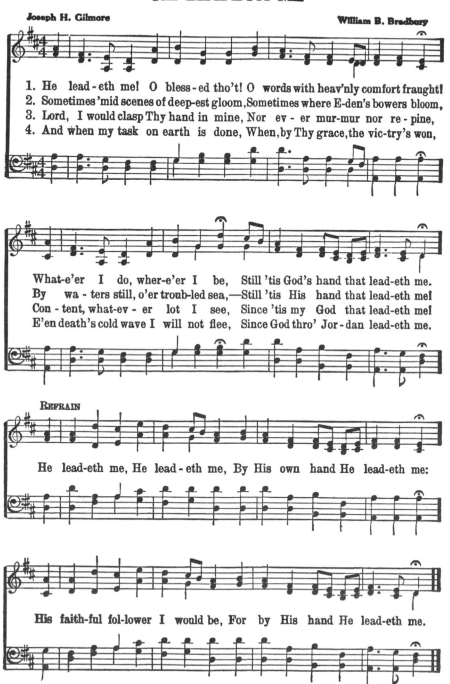

1. He lead-eth me! O bless-ed tho't! O words with heav'nly comfort fraught!
2. Sometimes 'mid scenes of deep-est gloom, Sometimes where E-den's bowers bloom,
3. Lord, I would clasp Thy hand in mine, Nor ev - er mur-mur nor re - pine,
4. And when my task on earth is done, When, by Thy grace, the vic-try's won,

What-e'er I do, wher-e'er I be, Still 'tis God's hand that lead-eth me.
By wa - ters still, o'er troub-led sea,—Still 'tis His hand that lead-eth me!
Con - tent, what-ev - er lot I see, Since 'tis my God that lead-eth me!
E'en death's cold wave I will not flee, Since God thro' Jor-dan lead-eth me.

REFRAIN

He lead-eth me, He lead-eth me, By His own hand He lead-eth me:

His faith-ful fol-lower I would be, For by His hand He lead-eth me.

156 OPEN MY EYES THAT I MAY SEE

Copyright, 1923. Renewal by H. F. Sayles, F. E. Hathaway, owner

C. H. S.

CHAS. H. SCOTT

1. O - pen my eyes, that I may see, Glimpses of truth Thou hast for me;
2. O - pen my ears, that I may hear, Voi - ces of truth Thou send-est clear;
3. O - pen my mouth and let me bear Glad - ly the warm truth ev - 'ry-where;

Place in my hands the won-der-ful key That shall unclasp, and set me free.
And while the wave-notes fall on my ear, Ev-'ry-thing false will dis - ap-pear.
O - pen my heart and let me prepare Love with Thy chil-dren thus to share.

Si-lent - ly now I wait for Thee, Read-y, my God, Thy will to see;
Si-lent - ly now I wait for Thee, Read-y, my God, Thy will to see;
Si-lent - ly now I wait for Thee, Read-y, my God, Thy will to see;

O - pen my eyes, il - lu - mine me, Spir - it di - vine!
O - pen my ears, il - lu - mine me, Spir - it di - vine!
O - pen my heart, il - lu - mine me, Spir - it di - vine! A - men.

By permission Mrs. F. E. Hathaway, 7814 Bennett Ave., Chicago

157 SPIRIT OF THE LIVING GOD

DANIEL IVERSON

DANIEL IVERSON

Spir-it of the liv-ing God, Now de-scend on me! Spir-it of the
liv-ing God, Now de-scend on me! Break me, melt me, mould me,
fill me! Spir-it of the liv-ing God, Now de-scend on me! A-men.

158 LORD OF ALL BEING THRONED AFAR

OLIVER WENDELL HOLMES

W. H. GLADSTONE

1. Lord of all be - ing, throned a - far, Thy glo-ry flames from sun and star;
2. Sun of our life, Thy quick-ening ray Sheds on our path the glow of day;
3. Our mid-night is Thy smile with-drawn; Our noon-tide is Thy gra-cious dawn;
4. Lord of all life, be - low, a - bove, Whose light is truth, whose warmth is love,
5. Grant us Thy breath to make us free, And kindling hearts that burn for Thee,

Cen-tre and soul of ev-ery sphere, Yet to each lov-ing heart how near.
Star of our hope, Thy soft-ened light Cheers the long watches of the night.
Our rain-bow arch, Thy mer-cy's sign; All, save the clouds of sin, are Thine.
Be-fore Thy ev - er blaz-ing throne We ask no lus-tre of our own.
Till all Thy liv - ing al - tars claim One ho-ly light, one heav'nly flame. A-men.

159 MASTER, THE TEMPEST IS RAGING

MARY A. BAKER

H. R. PALMER

1. Mas - ter, the tem-pest is rag - ing! The bil-lows are toss - ing high!
2. Mas - ter, with an-guish of spir - it I bow in my grief to - day;
3. Mas - ter, the ter - ror is o - ver, The el - e-ments sweet-ly rest;

The sky is o'er-shadowed with blackness, No shel - ter or help is nigh;
The depths of my sad heart are troub-led; O wak - en and save, I pray!
Earth's sun in the calm lake is mir-rored, And heaven's with-in my breast.

"Car - est Thou not that we per - ish?" How canst Thou lie a - sleep,
Tor-rents of sin and of an - guish Sweep o'er my sink - ing soul!
Lin - ger, O bless-ed Re-deem - er, Leave me a - lone no more;

When each moment so mad - ly is threat-'ning A grave in the an - gry deep?
And I per - ish! I per - ish, dear Mas - ter; O has - ten, and take con - trol!
And with joy I shall make the blest har - bor, And rest on the bliss - ful shore.

MASTER, THE TEMPEST IS RAGING

160 LOOK, YE SAINTS, THE SIGHT IS GLORIOUS

Thomas Kelly

Henry Smart

1 Look, ye saints, the sight is glo - rious, See the Man of
2. Crown the Sav - iour, an - gels, crown Him: Rich the tro - phies
3. Sin - ners in de - ris - ion crowned Him, Mock - ing thus the
4. Hark, those bursts of ac - cla - ma - tion! Hark, those loud tri -

Sor - rows now; From the fight re - turned vic - to - rious,
Je - sus brings; In the seat of pow'r en - throne Him,
Sav - iour's claim; Saints and an - gels crowd a - round Him,
um - phant chords! Je - sus takes the high - est sta - tion:

Ev - 'ry knee to Him shall bow: Crown Him, crown Him!
While the vault of heav - en rings: Crown Him, crown Him!
Own His ti - tle, praise His name: Crown Him, crown Him!
O what joy the sight af - fords! Crown Him, crown Him!

Crown Him, crown Him! Crowns be - come the Vic - tor's brow.
Crown Him, crown Him! Crown the Sav - iour King of kings.
Crown Him, crown Him! Spread a - broad the Vic - tor's fame.
Crown Him, crown Him! King of kings, and Lord of lords! A - men.

161 SAFE IN THE ARMS OF JESUS

FANNY J. CROSBY Copyright, property of Fannie T. Doane W. H. DOANE

1. Safe in the arms of Je - sus, Safe on His gen - tle breast, There by His
2. Safe in the arms of Je - sus, Safe from cor-rod - ing care, Safe from the
3. Je - sus, my heart's dear ref - uge, Je - sus has died for me; Firm on the

love o'er - shad - ed, Sweet-ly my soul shall rest. Hark ! 'tis the voice of
world's temp-ta - tions, Sin can-not harm me there. Free from the blight of
Rock of A - ges, Ev - er my trust shall be. Here let me wait with

an - gels, Borne in a song to me, O - ver the fields of glo - ry,
sor - row, Free from my doubts and fears; On - ly a few more tri - als,
pa - tience, Wait till the night is o'er; Wait till I see the morn - ing

CHORUS

O - ver the jas - per sea.........
On - ly a few more tears !..... } Safe in the arms of Je - sus, Safe on His
Break on the gold-en shore......

gen - tle breast, There by His love o'er - shad- ed, Sweetly my soul shall rest.

162 FATHER, IN HIGH HEAVEN DWELLING

GEORGE RAWSON   WILLIAM JACKSON

1. Fa - ther, in high heav - en dwell - ing, May our even - ing
2. This day's sins O par - don, Sa - viour, E - vil thoughts, per -
3. While the night dews are dis - til - ling, Ho - ly Ghost, each

song be tell - ing Of Thy mer - cy large and free;
verse be - hav - iour, En - vy, pride, and van - i - ty;
heart be fill - ing From Thine own in - fin - i - ty.

Through the day Thy love has fed us, Through the day Thy
From the world, the flesh, de - liv - er, Save us now, and
Soft - ly let the eyes be clos - ing, Lov - ing souls on

care has led us, With di - vin - est char - i - ty.
save us ev - er, O Thou Lamb of Cal - va - ry.
Thee re - pos - ing, Ev - er - bless - ed Trin - i - ty. A - men.

163   ARISE, MY SOUL, ARISE

CHARLES WESLEY   LEWIS EDSON

1. A - rise, my soul, a - rise; Shake off thy guilty fears; The bleed-ing Sac-ri-
2. He ev - er lives a - bove, For me to in - ter - cede; His all - re - deem-ing
3. Five bleed-ing wounds He bears, Re-ceived on Cal - va - ry, They pour ef - fect-ual
4. The Fa - ther hears Him pray, His dear a - noint-ed One; He can-not turn a -
5. My God is rec - on - ciled; His pard'ning voice I hear, He owns me for His

ARISE, MY SOUL, ARISE

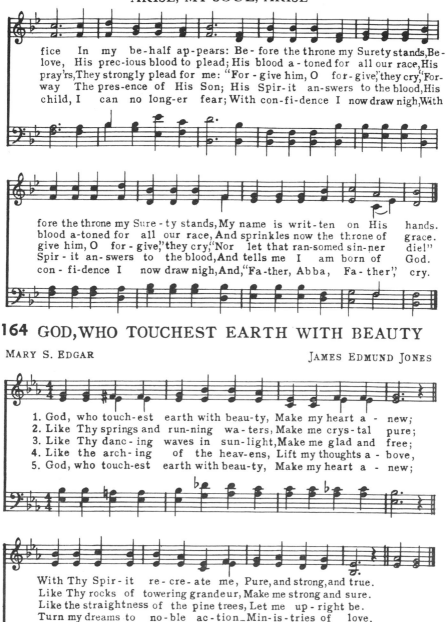

fice In my be-half ap-pears: Be- fore the throne my Surety stands,Be-
love, His prec-ious blood to plead; His blood a - toned for all our race,His
pray'rs,They strongly plead for me: "For - give him, O for - give,"they cry,"For-
way The pres-ence of His Son; His Spir-it an-swers to the blood,His
child, I can no long-er fear; With con-fi-dence I now draw nigh,With

fore the throne my Sure-ty stands,My name is writ-ten on His hands.
blood a-toned for all our race, And sprinkles now the throne of grace.
give him, O for - give,"they cry,"Nor let that ran-somed sin-ner die!"
Spir-it an-swers to the blood,And tells me I am born of God.
con-fi-dence I now draw nigh,And,"Fa-ther, Abba, Fa-ther," cry.

164 GOD, WHO TOUCHEST EARTH WITH BEAUTY

MARY S. EDGAR   JAMES EDMUND JONES

1. God, who touch-est earth with beau-ty, Make my heart a - new;
2. Like Thy springs and run-ning wa-ters, Make me crys-tal pure;
3. Like Thy danc-ing waves in sun-light, Make me glad and free;
4. Like the arch-ing of the heav-ens, Lift my thoughts a - bove,
5. God, who touch-est earth with beau-ty, Make my heart a - new;

With Thy Spir-it re - cre-ate me, Pure, and strong, and true.
Like Thy rocks of towering grandeur, Make me strong and sure.
Like the straightness of the pine trees, Let me up-right be.
Turn my dreams to no-ble ac-tion Min-is-tries of love.
Keep me ev - er by Thy Spir-it, Pure, and strong, and true. A - men.

NOW THANK WE ALL OUR GOD

Martin Rinkart
Tr. by Catherine Winkworth

Crüger's Praxis Pietatis Melica

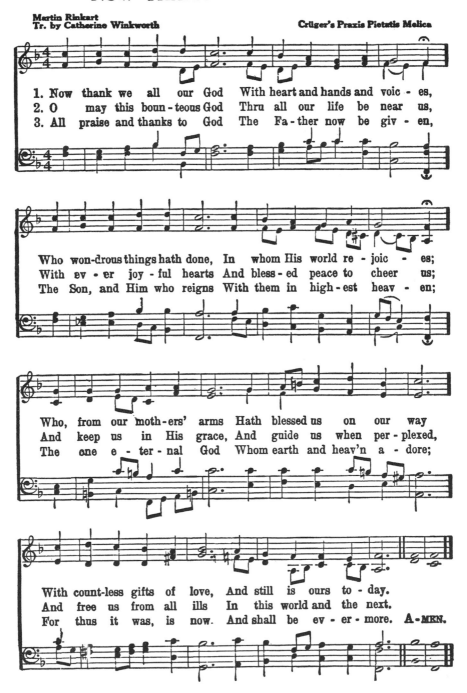

1. Now thank we all our God With heart and hands and voic - es,
2. O may this boun - teous God Thru all our life be near us,
3. All praise and thanks to God The Fa - ther now be giv - en,

Who won-drous things hath done, In whom His world re - joic - es;
With ev - er joy - ful hearts And bless - ed peace to cheer us;
The Son, and Him who reigns With them in high-est heav - en;

Who, from our moth-ers' arms Hath blessed us on our way
And keep us in His grace, And guide us when per - plexed,
The one e - ter - nal God Whom earth and heav'n a - dore;

With count-less gifts of love, And still is ours to - day.
And free us from all ills In this world and the next.
For thus it was, is now. And shall be ev - er - more. A - MEN.

166 O GOD, OUR HELP IN AGES PAST

Isaac Watts

William Croft

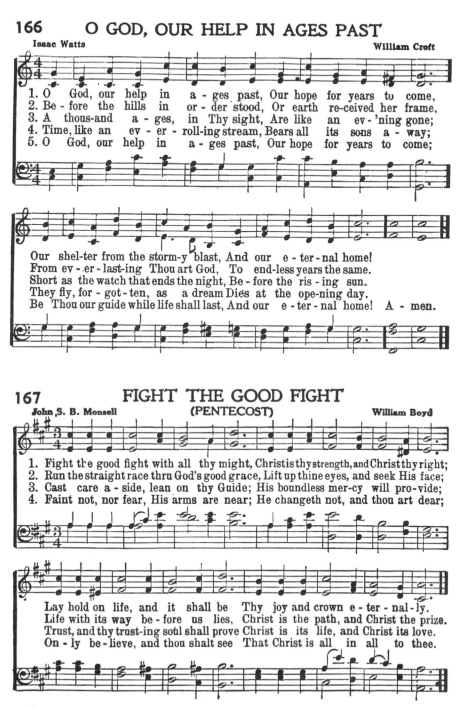

1. O God, our help in a - ges past, Our hope for years to come,
2. Be - fore the hills in or - der stood, Or earth re-ceived her frame,
3. A thous-and a - ges, in Thy sight, Are like an ev - 'ning gone;
4. Time, like an ev - er - roll-ing stream, Bears all its sons a - way;
5. O God, our help in a - ges past, Our hope for years to come;

Our shel-ter from the storm-y blast, And our e - ter - nal home!
From ev - er - last-ing Thou art God, To end-less years the same.
Short as the watch that ends the night, Be - fore the ris - ing sun.
They fly, for - got - ten, as a dream Dies at the ope-ning day.
Be Thou our guide while life shall last, And our e - ter - nal home! A - men.

167 FIGHT THE GOOD FIGHT
(PENTECOST)

John S. B. Monsell

William Boyd

1. Fight the good fight with all thy might, Christ is thy strength, and Christ thy right;
2. Run the straight race thru God's good grace, Lift up thine eyes, and seek His face;
3. Cast care a - side, lean on thy Guide; His boundless mer-cy will pro-vide;
4. Faint not, nor fear, His arms are near; He changeth not, and thou art dear;

Lay hold on life, and it shall be Thy joy and crown e - ter - nal-ly.
Life with its way be - fore us lies, Christ is the path, and Christ the prize.
Trust, and thy trust-ing soul shall prove Christ is its life, and Christ its love.
On - ly be - lieve, and thou shalt see That Christ is all in all to thee.

—by permission Novello & Co. Ltd.
London, England.

ALMOST PERSUADED

P. P. B.

P. P. Bliss

1. "Al-most per-suad-ed," now to be-lieve; "Al-most per-suad-ed,"
2. "Al-most per-suad-ed," come, come to-day; "Al-most per-suad-ed,"
3. "Al-most per-suad-ed," har-vest is past! "Al-most per-suad-ed,"

Christ to re-ceive; Seems now some soul to say, "Go, Spir-it,
turn not a-way; Je-sus in-vites you here, An-gels are
doom comes at last! "Al-most" can-not a-vail; "Al-most" is

go Thy way, Some more con-ven-ient day On Thee I'll call."
lin-g'ring near, Prayers rise from hearts so dear, O wan-d'rer, come.
but to fail! Sad, sad, that bit-ter wail, "Al-most," but lost!

ONLY TRUST HIM

J. H. S.

J. H. Stockton

1. Come, ev-'ry soul by sin op-pressed, There's mer-cy with the Lord,
2. For Je-sus shed His pre-cious blood, Rich bless-ings to be-stow;
3. Yes, Je-sus is the Truth, the Way, That leads you in-to rest:

And He will sure-ly give you rest By trust-ing in His Word.
Plunge now in-to the crim-son flood That wash-es white as snow.
Be-lieve in Him with-out de-lay, And you are ful-ly blest.

On - ly trust Him, on - ly trust Him, On - ly trust Him now;
He will save you, He will save you, He will (*Omit.* . . .) save you now.

170   WORK, FOR THE NIGHT IS COMING

ANNIE L. COGHILL   LOWELL MASON

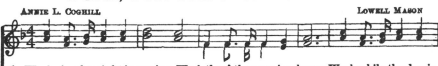

1. Work, for the night is coming, Work thro' the morning hours; Work while the dew is
2. Work, for the night is coming, Work thro' the sun-ny noon; Fill brightest hours with
3. Work, for the night is coming,   Under the sunset skies; While the bright tints are

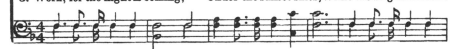

sparkling, Work 'mid springing flow'rs; Work when the day grows brighter, Work in the
la - bor, Rest comes sure and soon. Give ev-'ry fly-ing min-ute Something to
glow - ing, Work, for daylight flies. Work till the last beam fad-eth, Fadeth to

glow-ing sun;   Work, for the night is com - ing, When man's work is done.
keep in store: Work, for the night is com - ing, When man works no more.
shine no more; Work, while the night is dark'ning, When man's work is o'er.

DAY IS DYING IN THE WEST

MARY A. LATHBURY

WILLIAM F. SHERWIN

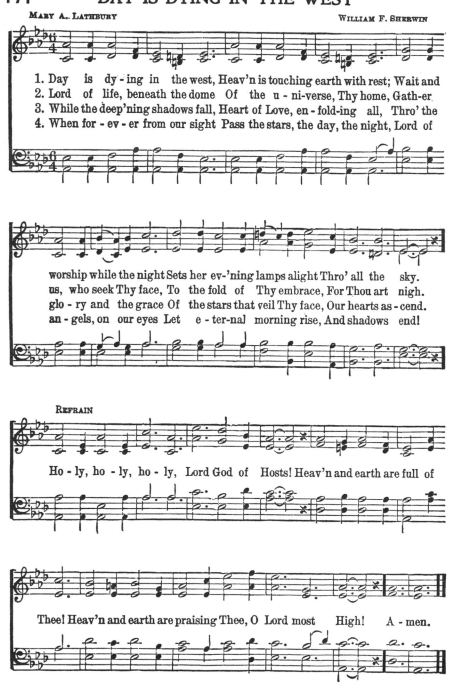

1. Day is dy-ing in the west, Heav'n is touching earth with rest; Wait and
2. Lord of life, beneath the dome Of the u-ni-verse, Thy home, Gath-er
3. While the deep'ning shadows fall, Heart of Love, en-fold-ing all, Thro' the
4. When for-ev-er from our sight Pass the stars, the day, the night, Lord of

worship while the night Sets her ev-'ning lamps alight Thro' all the sky.
us, who seek Thy face, To the fold of Thy embrace, For Thou art nigh.
glo-ry and the grace Of the stars that veil Thy face, Our hearts as-cend.
an-gels, on our eyes Let e-ter-nal morning rise, And shadows end!

REFRAIN

Ho-ly, ho-ly, ho-ly, Lord God of Hosts! Heav'n and earth are full of

Thee! Heav'n and earth are praising Thee, O Lord most High! A-men.

LOVE DIVINE

CHARLES WESLEY

JOHN ZUNDEL

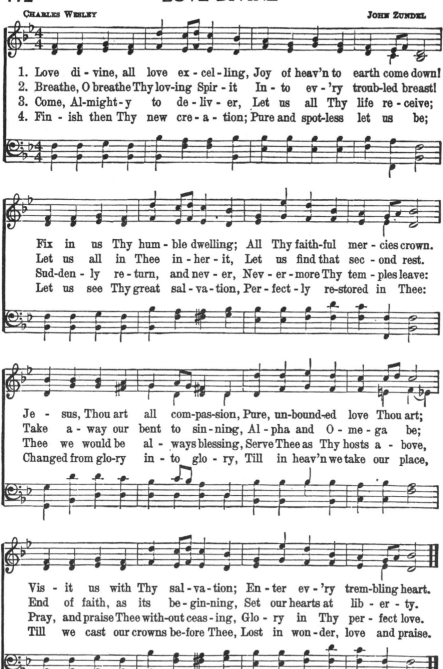

1. Love di - vine, all love ex - cel - ling, Joy of heav'n to earth come down!
2. Breathe, O breathe Thy lov-ing Spir - it In - to ev - 'ry troub-led breast!
3. Come, Al-might-y to de - liv - er, Let us all Thy life re - ceive;
4. Fin - ish then Thy new cre - a - tion; Pure and spot-less let us be;

Fix in us Thy hum - ble dwelling; All Thy faith-ful mer - cies crown.
Let us all in Thee in - her - it, Let us find that sec - ond rest.
Sud-den - ly re - turn, and nev - er, Nev - er-more Thy tem - ples leave:
Let us see Thy great sal - va-tion, Per - fect-ly re-stored in Thee:

Je - sus, Thou art all com-pas-sion, Pure, un-bound-ed love Thou art;
Take a - way our bent to sin-ning, Al - pha and O - me - ga be;
Thee we would be al - ways blessing, Serve Thee as Thy hosts a - bove,
Changed from glo-ry in - to glo - ry, Till in heav'n we take our place,

Vis - it us with Thy sal - va-tion; En - ter ev - 'ry trem-bling heart.
End of faith, as its be - gin-ning, Set our hearts at lib - er - ty.
Pray, and praise Thee with-out ceas - ing, Glo - ry in Thy per - fect love.
Till we cast our crowns be-fore Thee, Lost in won - der, love and praise.

GOD BE WITH YOU

173

J. E. RANKIN

W. G. TOMER

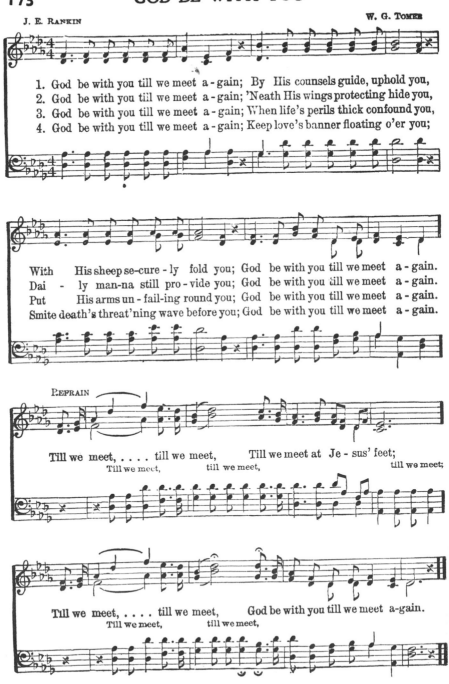

1. God be with you till we meet a-gain; By His counsels guide, uphold you,
2. God be with you till we meet a-gain; 'Neath His wings protecting hide you,
3. God be with you till we meet a-gain; When life's perils thick confound you,
4. God be with you till we meet a-gain; Keep love's banner floating o'er you;

With   His sheep se-cure-ly fold you; God be with you till we meet a-gain.
Dai - ly man-na still pro-vide you; God be with you till we meet a-gain.
Put   His arms un-fail-ing round you; God be with you till we meet a-gain.
Smite death's threat'ning wave before you; God be with you till we meet a-gain.

REFRAIN

Till we meet, ... till we meet,   Till we meet at Je-sus' feet;
Till we meet,   till we meet,   till we meet;

Till we meet, ... till we meet,   God be with you till we meet a-gain.
Till we meet,   till we meet,

LORD, I WANT TO BE A CHRISTIAN

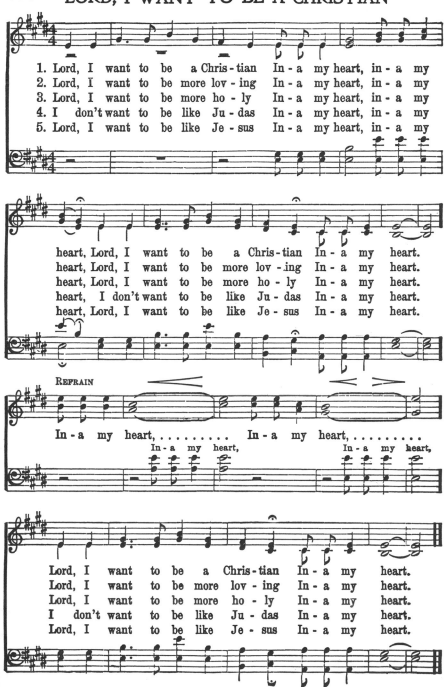

1. Lord, I want to be a Chris-tian In - a my heart, in - a my
2. Lord, I want to be more lov - ing In - a my heart, in - a my
3. Lord, I want to be more ho - ly In - a my heart, in - a my
4. I don't want to be like Ju - das In - a my heart, in - a my
5. Lord, I want to be like Je - sus In - a my heart, in - a my

heart, Lord, I want to be a Chris-tian In - a my heart.
heart, Lord, I want to be more lov -.ing In - a my heart.
heart, Lord, I want to be more ho - ly In - a my heart.
heart, I don't want to be like Ju - das In - a my heart.
heart, Lord, I want to be like Je - sus In - a my heart.

REFRAIN

In - a my heart, ... In - a my heart, ...
In - a my heart, In - a my heart,

Lord, I want to be a Chris-tian In - a my heart.
Lord, I want to be more lov - ing In - a my heart.
Lord, I want to be more ho - ly In - a my heart.
I don't want to be like Ju - das In - a my heart.
Lord, I want to be like Je - sus In - a my heart.

WERE YOU THERE?

1. Were you there when they cru - ci - fied my Lord? (were you there?)
2. Were you there when they nailed Him to the tree? (to the tree?)
3. Were you there when they pierced Him in the side? (in the side?)
4. Were you there when the sun re - fused to shine? (were you there?)
5. Were you there when they laid Him in the tomb? (in the tomb?)

Were you there when they cru - ci - fied my Lord? Oh! . . . .
Were you there when they nailed Him to the tree? Oh! . . . .
Were you there when they pierced Him in the side? Oh! . . . . . .
Were you there when the sun re - fused to shine? Oh! . . . . . . ;
Were you there when they laid Him in the tomb? Oh! . . . . . . ;

Some - times it caus - es me to trem - ble, trem - ble,
Some - times it caus - es me to trem - ble, trem - ble,
Some - times it caus - es me to trem - ble, trem - ble,
Some - times it caus - es me to trem - ble, trem - ble,
Some - times it caus - es me to trem - ble, trem - ble,

trem - ble, Were you there when they cru - ci - fied my Lord?
trem - ble, Were you there when they nailed Him to the tree?
trem - ble, Were you there when they pierced Him in the side?
trem - ble, Were you there when the sun re - fused to shine?
trem - ble, Were you there when they laid Him in the tomb?

SWING LOW

Swing low, sweet char - i - ot, Com - ing for to car - ry me

home; Swing low, sweet char - i - ot, Com - ing for to car - ry me home.
home; . . . .

1. I looked o - ver Jor - dan, and what did I see,
2. If you get there be - fore I do,
3. I'm some - times up, I'm some - times down,

Com - ing for to car - ry me home? A band of an - gels
Com - ing for to car - ry me home; Tell all my friends I'm
Com - ing for to car - ry me home; But still my soul feels

com - ing af - ter me, Com - ing for to car - ry me home.
com - ing too, Com - ing for to car - ry me home.
heav - en - ly bound, Com - ing for to car - ry me home.

177 EVERY TIME I FEEL THE SPIRIT

Negro Spiritual
Arr. by STANLEY L. OSBORNE

REFRAIN *Unison*

Ev-'ry time I feel the Spir-it Mov-ing in my heart, I will
pray. Ev-'ry time I feel the Spir - it Mov-ing
in my heart, I will pray.

Fine

1. Yes, I have tri-als and I have
2. But while He leads me I'll nev-er

D.C.

woe, And I have heart-aches here be-low.
fear, For I am shel-tered by all His care.

178 WE ARE CLIMBING JACOB'S LADDER

Negro Spiritual

SOLO   CHORUS

1. We are climb-ing Ja-cob's lad-der, We are climb-ing Ja-cob's
2. Ev-ery round goes high-er, high-er, Ev-ery round goes high-er,
3. Sin-ner, do you love my Je-sus? Sin-ner, do you love my
4. If you love Him, why not serve Him? If you love Him, why not
5. Do you think I'd make a sol-dier? Do you think I'd make a
6. Rise, shine, give God glo-ry! Rise, shine, give God

WE ARE CLIMBING JACOB'S LADDER

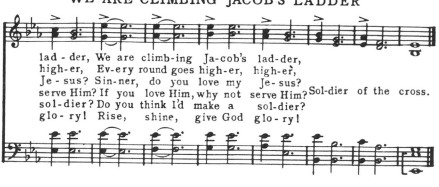

lad - der, We are climb-ing Ja-cob's lad-der,
high-er, Ev-er-y round goes high-er, high-er,
Je - sus? Sin-ner, do you love my Je - sus? Sol-dier of the cross.
serve Him? If you love Him, why not serve Him? Sol-dier of the cross.
sol-dier? Do you think I'd make a sol-dier?
glo - ry! Rise, shine, give God glo - ry!

179 MORE ABOUT JESUS

E. E. HEWITT   JNO. R. SWENEY

1. More about Je - sus would I know, More of His grace to oth - ers show;
2. More about Je - sus let me learn, More of His ho - ly will discern;
3. More about Je - sus; in His word, Hold-ing com-mun-ion with my Lord;
4. More about Je - sus on His throne, Riches in glo - ry all His own;

More of His sav-ing full-ness see, More of His love who died for me.
Spir - it of God, my teach-er be, Show-ing the things of Christ for me.
Hear-ing His voice in ev - 'ry line, Mak-ing each faithful say - ing mine.
More of His kingdom's sure in-crease; More of His com-ing, Prince of Peace.

D. S.—*More of His sav - ing full - ness see, More of His love who died for me.*

REFRAIN   *D. S*

More more a - bout Je - sus, More, more a - bout Je - sus;

180 STANDIN' IN THE NEED OF PRAYER

1. Not my brother, nor my sis - ter, but it's me, O Lord, Standin' in the need of pray'r;
2. Not the preacher, nor the dea-con, but it's me, O Lord, Standin' in the need of pray'r;
3. Not my father, nor my mother, but it's me, O Lord, Standin' in the need of pray'r;
4. Not the stranger, nor my neighbor, but it's me, O Lord, Standin' in the need of pray'r;

Not my brother, nor my sis - ter, but it's me, O Lord, Standin' in the need of pray'r.
Not the preacher, nor the dea-con, but it's me, O Lord, Standin' in the need of pray'r.
Not my father, nor my mother, but it's me, O Lord, Standin' in the need of pray'r.
Not the stranger, nor my neighbor, but it's me, O Lord, Standin' in the need of pray'r.

CHORUS

It's me, it's me, O Lord, Stand-in' in the need of pray'r;
It's me,

It's me, it's me, O Lord, Stand-in' in the need of pray'r.
It's me,

181 O CANADA!

"That True North"—*Tennyson*

Written by His Hon. R. Stanley Weir, D.C.L.
Recorder of Montreal

Melody by C. Lavallee
Harmonized by G. A. Grant Shaefer

mf Maestoso (Mixed voices)

1. O Can - a - da! Our home and native land! True pa-triot-love in
2. O Can - a - da! Where pines and maples grow. Great prairies spread and
3. O Can - a - da! Beneath thy shining skies May stal-wart sons and
4. Ru - ler supreme. Who hearest humble pray'r. Hold our Do - min - ion

all thy sons command. With glow-ing hearts we see thee rise The True North
lord-ly riv - ers flow. How dear to us thy broad domain. From East to
gen-tle maid-ens rise ; To keep thee steadfast thro' the years From East to
in Thy lov - ing care. Help us to find. O God in Thee A lasting,

strong and free ; And stand on guard. O Can - a - da. We stand on guard for thee.
West-ern sea! Thou land of hope for all who toil! Thou True North strong and free!
West-ern sea. Our own be - lov - ed na-tive land. Our True North strong and free.
rich re-ward. As wait-ing for the bet - ter day We ev - er stand on guard.

f Chorus *ad lib.*

O Can - a - da! Glo-rious and free! O Can - a - da! We stand on
guard for thee. O Can - a - da! We stand on guard for thee.

By permission Gordon V. Thompson Ltd., Toronto

182

God save the Queen

Attributed to John Bull (1652)
Arr. by Albert Ham

Andante moderato

1. God save our gra-cious Queen, Long live our
2. O Lord, our God, a-rise, Scat-ter her
3. Thy choic-est gifts in store, On her be

no-ble Queen, God save the_ Queen: Send her vic-
en-e-mies, And make them fall; Con-found their
pleased to pour; Long may she-reign: May she de-

to-ri-ous, Hap-py and glo-ri-ous,
pol-i-tics, Frus-trate their knav-ish tricks,
fend our laws, And ev-er give us cause

rit.

Long to_ reign ov-er us: God_ save the Queen.
On her our_ hopes we fix; God_ save us all.
To sing with heart and voice, God_ save the Queen.

MIZPAH

183

C. H. G.

Slowly

The Lord watch between me and thee When we are ab-sent one from the other. A-MEN.